DL　ＪＤIES

SOCIAL ATTITUDES AND AGRICULTURAL PRODUCTIVITY
IN CENTRAL AFRICA

BY
JEAN BONVIN

DEVELOPMENT CENTRE
OF THE ORGANISATION FOR ECONOMIC CO-OPERATION AND DEVELOPMENT

Pursuant to article 1 of the Convention signed in Paris on 14th December, 1960, and which came into force on 30th September, 1961, the Organisation for Economic Co-operation and Development (OECD) shall promote policies designed:

- to achieve the highest sustainable economic growth and employment and a rising standard of living in Member countries, while maintaining financial stability, and thus to contribute to the development of the world economy;
- to contribute to sound economic expansion in Member as well as non-member countries in the process of economic development; and
- to contribute to the expansion of world trade on a multilateral, non-discriminatory basis in accordance with international obligations.

The Signatories of the Convention on the OECD are Austria, Belgium, Canada, Denmark, France, the Federal Republic of Germany, Greece, Iceland, Ireland, Italy, Luxembourg, the Netherlands, Norway, Portugal, Spain, Sweden, Switzerland, Turkey, the United Kingdom and the United States. The following countries acceded subsequently to this Convention (the dates are those on which the instruments of accession were deposited): Japan (28th April, 1964), Finland (28th January, 1969), Australia (7th June, 1971) and New Zealand (29th May, 1973).

The Socialist Federal Republic of Yugoslavia takes part in certain work of the OECD (agreement of 28th October, 1961).

The Development Centre of the Organisation for Economic Co-operation and Development was established by decision of the OECD Council on 23rd October, 1962.

The purpose of the Centre is to bring together the knowledge and experience available in Member countries of both economic development and the formulation and execution of general policies of economic aid; to adapt such knowledge and experience to the actual needs of countries or regions in the process of development and to put the results at the disposal of the countries by appropriate means.

The Centre has a special and autonomous position within the OECD which enables it to enjoy scientific independence in the execution of its task. Nevertheless, the Centre can draw upon the experience and knowledge available in the OECD in the development field.

Publié en français sous le titre :

CHANGEMENTS SOCIAUX
ET PRODUCTIVITÉ AGRICOLE
EN AFRIQUE CENTRALE

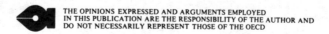

This study draws on unfamiliar sources of data to examine the structural problems of traditional farming in Africa. Its innovative approach shows that close attention to cultural factors is crucial for understanding why change is resisted and selecting the course of action most likely to promote development.

Also available

MEETING FOOD NEEDS IN A CONTEXT OF CHANGE by Hartmut Schneider (October 1984)
(41 84 03 1) ISBN 92-64-12623-6   150 pages   £6.50   US$13.00   F65.00

MANAGING INFORMATION FOR RURAL DEVELOPMENT PROJECTS by Nicolas Imboden (August 1980)
(41 80 03 1) ISBN 92-64-12039-4   98 pages   £2.90   US$6.50   F26.00

SELF-HELP AND POPULAR PARTICIPATION IN RURAL WATER SYSTEMS by Duncan Miller (April 1980)
(41 80 01 1) ISBN 92-64-12027-0   150 pages   £4.00   US$9.00   F36.00

To be published:
PROJECT AID: LIMITATIONS AND ALTERNATIVES, by Bernard Lecomte

Prices charged at the OECD Bookshop.

*THE OECD CATALOGUE OF PUBLICATIONS and supplements will be sent free of charge
on request addressed either to OECD Publications Service,
2, rue André-Pascal, 75775 PARIS CEDEX 16, or to the OECD Sales Agent in your country.*

LIST OF CONTENTS

Part One

ANALYSIS: AGRICULTURE AND THE RURAL STRUCTURES IN BURUNDI

LIST OF TABLES

The following tables were calculated from data gathered during the enquiry carried out in 1977.

LIST OF MAPS AND FIGURES

ACKNOWLEDGEMENTS

The successful completion of the research is due, on the one hand, to the support given by the Direction de la Coopération au Développement et de l'Aide Humanitaire of the Swiss Département fédéral des Affaires étrangères which financed the fieldwork and the processing of the data and, on the other, to the support from the University of Burundi and the national authorities who did much to encourage and facilitate the research. They deserve the warmest thanks.

The students from the University of Burundi who participated actively in the fieldwork also deserve our gratitude.

PREFACE

The Development Centre is paying special attention to the agricultural problems of the low-income countries and has been making a number of studies of the subject, in particular a research programme on the relationship between macro-economic polices and agricultural performance. This present work is in the same general line, since it provides a detailed analysis of the agricultural and rural structures of an African country, namely Burundi.

There are two parts: the first is a case study of the present situation of farmers in three rural areas of Burundi; the second part describes in some detail the method of enquiry in the hope that it may serve as a theoretical and practical model for similar research in other parts of the world. The principal aim of the study was to establish the basic data required for working out a development policy centred on an increase in agricultural production to a level capable of ensuring an adequate and balanced diet for the population, and at the same time providing the surpluses needed for the diversification of the economy.

The case study, based on a socio-economic enquiry covering 1 655 farmers, was intended to throw light, for example, on the abandonment by farmers of land they had been allotted in the Rusizi plain, where large-scale production of commercial crops (cotton and rice) had been organised with the help of foreign aid. This problem is as crucial for the local authorities as it is for the regional development corporations and for the external aid agencies, which have invested considerable human and financial resources in projects of this kind. It is even more crucial for the farmers themselves, who had left their ancestral homelands in the hope of a better life. And yet these vast holdings known as "paysannats" (peasant communities), seemed at first sight to offer ideal conditions of production, produce marketing and infrastructure (health, education, roads, housing).

To shed light on these questions, the author sets out the facts of economic life for the farming families, analyses the farming methods, and describes the systems of purchase or transfer of property and goods and of property rights. He presents a complete inventory of agricultural production, compares yields obtained by different farming methods and comes finally, after a series of highly significant statistical calculations, to a multivariate analysis, region by region. This makes it possible to identify relevant features in the transformation of rural life and bring out the hidden mechanisms of economic and social change. The research is therefore dynamic in character, in the sense that the enquiry and its results are capable of providing the basis for a new strategy for the harmonious development of rural society.

The study shows clearly that agricultural development can be achieved only through increases in productivity. In a country where economic activities outside agriculture are virtually non-existent, the need is to promote food crops while at the same time maintaining the cash crops intended for export. It is not only a matter of feeding an increasingly numerous population living on land which is already densely populated, but one of simultaneously creating non-agricultural activities capable of absorbing the excess manpower. Only if substantial surpluses are produced in agriculture will it be possible to achieve economic diversification and thus create new jobs. With this aim in mind, the installation of appropriate infrastructure for production (feeder roads, tools, light machinery), and for health and education and the introduction of a strict pricing policy are shown to be indispensable. One of the interesting aspects of the study is the concrete proposals it contains, as well as the range of possible types of intervention by the institutions involved.

The techniques used to obtain an understanding of Burundi's rural structure have provided material which is both abundant and highly significant concerning social change in rural areas. Throughout the successive stages of data collection – observation, proverb-based interviews and the quantitative enquiry – particular attention was paid to the need to respect the imperative requirements of research. The rules of scientific enquiry, aimed at revealing the full complexity of the truth and its many interwoven components, were scrupulously adhered to.

Another specific feature of the study to be noted is that its approach is essentially individualistic and anthropological, since the interviews were focused on people rather than groups, with the conclusions at group level drawn from indirect a posteriori reasoning. Its originality lies in the fact that the farmers and interviewers came from the same background, so that the enquiry took place entirely within the carefully chosen groups. This provided not only social, but linguistic homogeneity; the use of local dialect and proverbs brought the enquiry down to a human scale, and made it possible to apprehend the farmer's real life situation, both material and moral, and, in particular, his economic thinking.

Such an approach, based on real-life experience, shows, among other things, that the analysis of cultural phenomena is fundamental to an understanding of the nature and reasons of resistance to change and to establishing the most appropriate basis and methods for achieving development. In the final analysis, however, – and this has to be stressed – while this book claims to present a global picture of the phenomena and has essentially economic objectives, it is mainly addressed to the people involved in development as a basis for taking informed decisions.

Just FAALAND
President
of the OECD Development Centre
November 1985

POLITICAL MAP OF BURUNDI

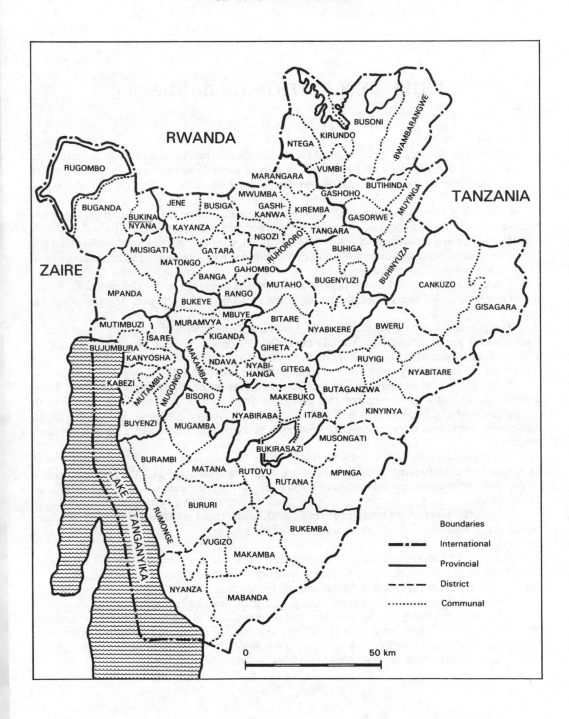

BRIEF DESCRIPTION OF BURUNDI

Situated in the Great Lakes region of Central Africa astride latitude 3° South, Burundi is spread over 27 834 sq. km (2 000 consisting of part of Lake Tanganyika). It is a land-locked country, bordered on the North by Rwanda, on the East by Zaire, on the South and East by Tanzania.

Formerly a German colony (1896-1916), later a mandated territory and then a trust territory under the Kingdom of Belgium, before acquiring independence on 1st July 1962, Burundi has been a republic since 1966. It is now divided into 15 provinces administered by a Governor, the provinces themselves being divided into arrondissements and communes (and locally into hill-districts and zones).

The climate is tropical in the plain and temperate at higher levels (from 1 500 to over 2 000 metres), with annual rainfall varying between 1 000 and 1 500 mm depending on the region.

The population was estimated to be 4.4 million in 1982, with an annual growth rate of 2.65 per cent per year, and is essentially rural (95 per cent). Average population density is 170 inhabitants per sq. km., but is as high as 350 in some regions. GDP per head was 194 dollars in 1982; the daily wage for a worker is of the order of 1.20 dollars.

Burundi lives off agriculture, with coffee providing most of the export receipts. Food crops (cassava and sorghum, maize, rice and groundnuts) are of considerable importance in the agriculture of a country which is still largely a subsistence economy. Efforts are being made, with the help of international organisations, to extend the irrigated area and train rural leaders.

The country is hilly and dotted with rugo (family enclosures) separated by a patchwork of fields and pastures. Banana trees and beans are to be found on every hill, the latter being the staple food and the former used to make a strong beer which is consumed in large quantities by the Barundi.

Livestock makes only a small contribution, although there are substantial herds, but not raised for slaughter. Cattle are a sign of wealth and play an important part in social relations.

Most of the fuel consumed by households is wood. Burundi, which depends mainly on Zaire to meet its electricity needs, is at present building hydro-electric power stations to make itself independent in this respect by the end of the decade.

Burundi's mineral resources are still largely unexploited, apart from sand for glassmaking. Studies now being made concern the exploitation of certain mineral resources (phosphates, carbonalites, nickel, sands, clays) and the improvement of existing operations (gold, tin, bastnasite, tungsten). A few food and textile factories have been established in Bujumbura, where there are also some factories for metallic structures.

INTRODUCTION

It may be useful at this point to define the general objective of the research and to describe the general problem underlying it. The study sets out to show that the future of rural societies is by no means yet decided. There is clear evidence of cracks in the former structure, but resistance to outside influence remains very strong. It is dangerous to accept the thesis of modernistic theoreticians who see the Western model of evolution as the one which all societies inevitably must follow; it is equally risky to adopt unchallenged the assumptions of those theoreticians who take a historical and global approach according to which rural societies undergoing change necessarily fall under the domination of capitalism. Nevertheless, the principle underlying the theories put forward by both these groups is of fundamental importance, namely, – as history has long since taught us – that social phenomena must be treated globally, that no detail can be ignored, that the smallest fact may be of great importance, and that the economic factor is dialectically related at all times to other social aspects. But, in addition, the study sets out to show that although everything in a living organism is inter-related, there is nothing to show that economic factors are the prime mover in all social change – still less that they must be the principal concern of any society.

This, in short, is the perennially topical rationale underlying the study. In fact, in spite of efforts made over many decades to improve agricultural production in the developing countries, the development agents, and particularly the agronomists, run up against stubborn resistance and are obliged to seek sociological explanations for the difficulties encountered in the more modern parts of the agricultural sector. The main aim of the research was therefore to establish the fundamental data necessary for working out an effective development policy, centred on an increase in agricultural output.

It was therefore first necessary to choose the analytical methods, the theoretical framework, the basic concepts and the sophisticated measurement tools needed to build the detailed argumentation concerning the transformation of rural life or the shift from one type of production to another. This is why, without losing sight of the analysis of production factors, the study tried to pick out the reality at a number of different levels, using extremely detailed observation and multivariate comparisons, in order to reach a profound understanding of the basic structure. The approach here was more one of applied economics than of trying to develop a new economic theory.

The advocates of modernism, by favouring the urban sector over the rural, have discredited agrarian society by treating it as essentially parasitic. Some of them can nevertheless be commended for having been able to discern the links between apparently unrelated factors such as religion, schooling, mobility, productivity, class structure, hierarchy, law, kindred relationships, age structures and the trading and monetary systems. Unfortunately, all approaches of this kind and those which constitute the logical next steps involve purely static models which take into account neither the historical evolution of societies nor the accompanying structural changes. The result is a closed system in which the notions of power relationships or of domination are entirely absent. Yet, as is well known, these are the factors that determine the process of development and/or underdevelopment and the form it takes. Change is not brought about by simply adding or subtracting discrete elements; tradition is conditioned by modernity just as modern ideas need to take account of tradition if they are to be accepted; the two are inextricably linked.

The historical-global approach, on the other hand, has the merit of paying particular attention to the interdependences in the way the various factors change over time. In particular, this approach maintains that there is a hierarchical structuring of basic concepts; in other words, that production relationships evolve as a result of the evolution of the productive forces and inevitably contain the seeds of class conflict. (In this case, it is land and titles to land which are shown to play the central role.) This approach has the further merit of highlighting the exact role to be attributed in any social evolution to ideological factors of various kinds (religious, cultural, juridical, political), or in short the entire superstructure. Finally, this approach shows clearly the mechanisms which, in a given social context, bring about the changes in production relationships (moving from pre-capitalist to capitalist forms of production), thus demonstrating the consequences for domestic and world markets and for the national monetary and trading systems.

What factors and mechanisms set in motion the shift from one stage to another? What indicators enable one to understand this phenomenon of change in the rural sector and in the rest of society? Are the social changes accompanied by an increase in the intensity of agricultural production and, if so, who benefits? Finally, what implications does the increase in production have for society as a whole?

These, in substance, are the questions discussed in this book. The reasoning, to remain intelligible, uses classic concepts of economics and sociology.

In research of this kind, it is not enough merely to assemble the largest possible number of facts and then study the dynamic relations between them. Just as facts can only be understood in conjunction with some underlying theory, so a dialectical relationship must emerge between the theory and the empirical reality in the field. The manifold interrelationships between the various social groups within the economic system require methods of observation and analysis capable of throwing light on the whole.

In studying the rural structure in Burundi, special efforts were made to go beyond a simple exposition of the facts by placing them in a theoretical framework making it possible to examine the many and complex relationships which give meaning to these facts and to bring out the consistencies and linkages within the system. The starting-points were the existing state of the productive forces (consisting of the principal means of production such as land, animals, tools and agricultural equipment and the labour force), agricultural production itself and the resulting manifold social relationships. The observation process was built around the problems of agricultural development. In this way, the classic approach, after incorporation of a series of indispensable safeguards, provided the basis for an in-depth study.

However, because they were only too well aware of the intricacy of social reality and the complex internal dynamics of any change involving facts or people, the authors rejected any idea that economic factors provide a unilateral or causal explanation of the shaping of social reality. Although the study was based on economic aspects, it never lost sight of the daily reality of the life of the Burundian peasant and of its special features. He is not alone in the world, however, even though he remains bound by his condition as a farmer and a Burundian farmer, at that. The methodology described in Part II, whose application to Burundi constitutes Part I, is capable of being transposed to other peasant societies and to other countries.

The introduction of cash crops, to a greater or lesser extent, by the colonisers brought about certain social and cultural changes; but the importance of these crops depends in turn on some degree of sustained action on the part of the national authorities through the appropriate regulation and supervision of production. Nevertheless, the insertion of the producers into the world economy through cash crops such as coffee and cotton exposes them to some extent to the constraints and the logic enforced by the outside world, which is then able to impose its own standards and organise production to suit its own interests.

The analysis had therefore to take account of all these requirements. For the approach itself, a number of techniques often used in economics or the social sciences were deliberately rejected. Certain field experimental techniques (such as participatory observation) might have helped to reach a better understanding of the mechanisms of social change in rural areas. But they raised the problem of how, in an African society, one can prevent external influences on the field of observation, once the experimental method and the control groups have been established. Nor did it seem possible to answer vital and urgent questions affecting today's farmers by using experimental techniques which produce reliable results only in the long term.

The method applied in this research should at least be given credit for a bold attack on the problems, for raising real-life questions, for indicating viable solutions, for suggesting possible concrete paths to rural development, for consistently placing the Burundi farmer at the centre of the study and giving him his full dignity, his true weight in the social order, and the right to be heard.

Part One

ANALYSIS:
AGRICULTURE AND THE RURAL STRUCTURES IN BURUNDI

(For the convenience of the reader, a short methodological introduction is given before proceeding to detailed analysis of the results. Part Two gives full information concerning the methods used and the reader may therefore wish to refer to it first. The statistical data presented in the tables are the results of a field enquiry carried out in 1977.)

I. THE SETTING FOR THE STUDY AND THE METHODS USED

The preparation of the actual study (sampling, submission and processing of questionnaires) was preceded by a long ground-clearing period aimed at ensuring that the techniques to be used were properly suited to the economic and social realities of the subject.

The first stage consisted of a methodical examination of a whole series of documents, dealing with: the physical background (maps and aerial photographs[1]), the population (this information was available only at regional and communal levels), the nature of society in the colonial period and, finally, agriculture and the rural economy. Documents from colonial times give very interesting information on cultivation and livestock methods. Studies made at the time by agronomists and economists provide precise and useful information on such questions as the relationships between inputs and final production, the farming calendar, farming methods, marketing of crops, and the structure of household expenses, but almost exclusively in relation to cash crops.

The second stage consisted of a series of semi-directive interviews. In order to make the concepts of the research understandable, these were interpreted in terms of traditional proverbs, to be closer to the farmers' own language, but to avoid getting replies which simply conformed to the social values which the farmer attributed to the interviewer, some contradictory traditional proverbs were thrown into the discussion[2]. Certain elements of the proverb with particular significance for the approach used in the study were then reintroduced and explored more deeply through a series of open-ended questions, in order to bring out concrete experiences taken from real life. These qualitative interviews were carried out with the help of interpreter-interviewers who were previously given intensive training. Chosen from people living in rural areas and in close touch with their thinking, they were able to gain the farmers' confidence, but at the same time to think in sufficiently abstract terms to understand the ideas underlying the study. This stage of the research was limited to about ten

19

semi-directive in-depth interviews, obtaining answers from about thirty individuals. Transcripts were made of the interviews, which were then translated at the University and the resulting texts submitted to a content analysis. The final questionnaire used in the study was based on the results.

The sampling technique was chosen for its suitability for the subject of the study, namely the changes in the economic and social structures in the agricultural sector. With this aim in mind, the three regions chosen were each at a different stage of the transition from subsistence to commercial farming. These were: Bubanza (the Rusizi plain), Ngozi and Ruyigi. It was in Bubanza that change was most evident. This region is entirely divided by a grid-pattern of roads into large geometric areas. The peasant communities inside these areas comprise a number of small holdings side-by-side, each of identical acreage. Within each holding a given area is earmarked for cotton or rice and crop rotation is organised to suit this particular crop. Since independence, however, many farmers no longer submit to the discipline imposed by these holdings and even sometimes abandon them entirely, in spite of the advantages of what would normally be considered the best available infrastructure and support (roads, irrigation canals, advice from agronomists, dispensaries, schools, etc.) In the other two regions, agriculture is still traditional, but in Ngozi coffee is grown on a large scale, which is not true of Ruyigi. Also, Ngozi is the most densely-populated region of Burundi, with 286 inhabitants to the square kilometre, while Ruyigi is the least (69 inhabitants to the square kilometre) and has substantial reserves of cultivable land. The three regions chosen therefore represent the various extremes existing in Burundi agriculture.

The number of people to be interviewed in each region was set at 500, counting only the adult heads of household, in order to be able to carry out multivariate analysis within each region. For this, 500 is a minimum figure, because with three variables examined simultaneously and with three possible values for each, the average number of observations per cell is still theoretically less than 20. The number was not chosen in relation to the weight of population in each region (500 people is equivalent to 4 per cent of the adult males in Ngozi but 10 per cent in the two other regions).

The sampling for Bubanza was based on the population of the peasant communities and not the total population. In contrast, in the two other regions, sampling was carried out at three successive levels: the commune, the hill-district, and then the inhabitants within each hill-district selected. The choice of commune was based on population density. Within each region, the densest and the least dense commune were chosen; next, the commune with median density and finally the two with densities midway between the two extremes and the median. Then within each commune five hill-districts were chosen by random sampling, as were the individuals in each hill-district, using the Administration's files and records of heads of household[3]. In all cases a few more names were drawn than were actually required, in order to make up for the inevitable gaps (people absent, ill, migrated, etc.). In addition, the actual number of persons interviewed was 1 655, or rather more than 1 500, in order to allow for unusable questionnaires.

In the drafting of the questionnaire, care was taken to include non-economic and qualitative variables. In this way, account was taken of such factors as religious persuasion, education, parents' ambitions for the schooling of their children, relations with the administrative authorities, social mobility, the importance attached to money and to cash crops, and opinions on what constituted a fair return for services of various kinds.

The initial questionnaire, consisting of 540 questions, was tested in advance in each of the regions (on about 15 peasants in each). The results were used in drafting the final version, with 395 questions. This pilot enquiry was particularly useful for selecting the indicators with the highest degree of reliability and relevance. For example, in the part dealing with politics and religion, it was possible to drop several questions because they produced almost identical results. The most important modifications consisted of a refinement of the section dealing with agricultural production and the amount of work put into each crop.

To facilitate recollection, questions on production, consumption, sales and expenses were asked in four stages, starting with what was freshest in the person's memory and proceeding to what was farthest off in time. Questions on the time devoted to each crop distinguished between the type of work and also the type of labour (family member or outsider, adult or child). To measure the amount of work, it was necessary to abandon the units used in the pilot questionnaire and adopt only those which corresponded to the peasants' own practices. The experience of the pilot enquiry also led to the adoption of the number of paces of length and breadth as the best measure of area.

The final version of the questionnaire was divided into five parts: the family of the respondent, the means of production, the production itself, the household budget and savings and, finally, social, political and religious relationships and the way change is perceived.

The questions on the extended family (number, age and civil status of its members, their migrations, professional and social mobility, etc.) made it easier to delimit the family in the narrow sense – the nuclear family inhabiting a single dwelling. It is the family in this latter sense – the conjugal family – which constituted the basic unit for the enquiry and it was this unit whose history and composition were established by the questionnaire.

The means of production consist of the pieces of land cultivated by the household, the animals, the tools and the labour. The questions on the pieces of land were highly diverse, dealing with their areas, the way they were acquired, the social implications of the transactions, the forms of payment for rented land, the titles to property, conflicts concerning land, views on the concentration of land ownership, etc. All the usual questions on production techniques were also included. Those concerning the animals dealt with all aspects of the question, including, for example, food tabus, the social implications of the various transactions, and relationships between livestock activities and cultivation.

The questions on production made a clear distinction between cash crops and food crops. In each case, details were requested on the amount of labour put into each type of product, the quantities produced, the way they were marketed, and the significance of these crops for the farmer.

The monetary expenditures of the household were broken down in the questionnaire between consumption goods and production inputs. It went on to detail the expenditures under each particular heading. Savings were broken down into free saving, forced saving and hoarding.

The last section of the questionnaire dealt with religious, political and social factors, as well as the influence of tradition on the household's behaviour and its perception of social change.

Although the questionnaire was long and very detailed, it was not entirely exhaustive: it contained no question on housing, a variable which is both significant and easy to measure. In addition, certain data on social factors, and on household industries, cultivation techniques and livestock, were not obtained with the accuracy and detail one could have wished.

The fieldwork required painstaking preparation, considerable resources and strict supervision. The interviewers, 47 students each of whom was a native of one of the three regions, were given an intensive two-week formal training beforehand. The necessary contacts were made in advance with the political and administrative authorities and the administrator of the commune was associated with the drawing of the names of people to be interviewed, so that it would be clear that the choice was being made on precise scientific criteria, regardless of any other considerations. All possible precautions were taken to ensure the acceptance of the enquiry by all the people concerned, both among the authorities and the farmers. Two supervisors, assisted by one or other of the student researchers, kept a constant watch on the fieldwork. From time to time, there were repeat interviews, carried out by a supervisor assisted by a researcher from outside the normal group. The main aim was to see whether the respondent again gave the same replies to the same questions; in addition, the results of the repeat interview helped to polish the training of the researchers. An enquiry of this scope requires a rigid and clear system for keeping track of the sending out and return of the questionnaires, as well as of the persons to be interviewed. This was done for each group by means of a card index kept up to date by an interviewer designated for the purpose.

Following the enquiries on the ground, the questionnaires were tested for consistency. A group specially created for this task carried out 82 tests which led to the elimination of 67 questionnaires out of 1 655 because of multiple and repeated inconsistencies. Since the remaining 1 588 questionnaires contained 395 questions with 2 631 possible answers, this meant roughly 4 million items of information, obviously needing a computer for their analysis. Each questionnaire required 70 cards. This high figure resulted from the large number of open or open-ended questions in cases where the lack of basic information prevented the preparation of closed questions. A small group of reliable students carried out the coding, while the supervisors themselves were responsible for the coding of answers to all the open or open-ended questions. The coding was then subjected to three successive checks covering the totality of the replies. Once the cards had been punched, the whole data base was transferred to magnetic tape at the electronic computing centre of the Swiss Federal Administration in Berne.

A first analysis provided the normal measures of dispersion for each of the variables. The extreme values of an abnormal character were checked against the original questionnaire to make sure that there had been no error in the coding. In many cases the various possible replies were grouped together, leading to a substantial reduction in the number of variables, from the original 2 631 to 564, of which 129 were used in the multi-variate analysis.

Certain variables, such as the real income of the household, were constructed from tens, or even hundreds, of observed ones. For example, 353 original variables were needed for the calculation of the net income (186 for the gross income plus 167 for the variables concerning running costs). Other variables constructed in a similar way included: productivity per hectare, productivity per active member of household, capital-intensity per hectare or per active member (number of tools *times* price of tools *divided by* number of hectares or of productive adults), labour intensity per hectare of available land (effective or theoretical)[4], gains or losses from employing someone from outside the household (value of a day's production by an adult member of the household *minus* the daily remuneration of the non-member).

The techniques index took account of three basic techniques aimed at improving productivity (use of fertilizer or manure, use of selected seeds, anti-erosion practices) with four values, 0 to 3, depending on the number of these techniques used by the farmer.

The degree of home consumption was calculated in two different ways: either as the ratio between the value of the food consumed in the household and the value of total agricultural production or as the ratio between the area devoted to food crops and total area.

Similarly, the degree of integration into the world economy was calculated on the basis of the ratio of the value of production (or the area) of coffee or cotton to the total value (or area) for the holding.

An attempt was also made to assign an index to the strength of tradition, using five elements which should theoretically reflect the attachment of the person interviewed to tradition: the consumption of mutton (a very strong food tabu); the worship of Kiranga;

ancestor-worship; attitudes to witch-doctors; and use of traditional medicine[5]. The final analysis of the results was carried out by the usual methods: factor analysis, multiple regression and breakdown.

These indications concerning the techniques used and the characteristics of the questionnaire show the care which was taken at every stage to respect the rules of scientific research while at the same time attempting to grasp all the diversity of the economic and social realities of the subject. It was for this precise reason that it was considered indispensable to introduce the numerous non-economic variables, sometimes qualitative in nature (social, political and religious relationships; opinions on a fair wage, on conflicts over ownership, etc.). It turned out to be impossible to grasp and understand the evolution of Burundi agriculture without placing it in a much broader context than that of the rural economy.

II. AGRARIAN STRUCTURES

Unlike several of its neighbours, such as Zaire, Tanzania or Kenya, where large holdings of a capitalist type play an appreciable role in agriculture, Burundi has only small traditional holdings, known as amatongo. These are made up of several small plots often next to the farmer's hut. The farmers are independent producers working for the most part on their own land. In fact, in the three regions studied, the proportion of farmers working exclusively on their own land ranged from 81 per cent to 90 per cent, while only 2 per cent to 5 per cent rented more than 30 per cent of the land they cultivated.

A. The agricultural holdings

1. The distribution of holdings by size

Table 1 summarises the basic data on the distribution of farm holdings. Two facts stand out. For the three regions together, the size of the majority of holdings turned out to be very small: one-third were of less than one hectare and three-quarters had less than 4 hectares. There was a sharp difference, however, between the Bubanza region, where 70 per cent of the

Table 1. **Distribution of holdings by size and by region**

Size of holding in hectares	Percentage of holdings			Total	
	Bubanza	Ngozi	Ruyigi	%	Number of respondents
0.00 – 0.49	3.2	15.5	19.6	12.2	195
0.50 – 0.99	13.5	23.3	21.0	19.0	301
1.00 – 1.99	13.0	27.5	26.0	21.6	343
2.00 – 3.99	33.3	18.6	15.5	23.1	367
≥4.00	36.9	15.1	17.9	24.1	382
Total	100.0	100.0	100.0	100.0	1 588

farmers had more than 2 hectares, and Ngozi and Ruyigi, where the corresponding proportion was only one-third.

Taking the two homogeneous groups separately, Bubanza on the one hand and the two other provinces on the other, it is clear that the peasant communities have exerted a decisive influence on agrarian structure in Bubanza. But other demographic and social factors have also had an effect. The impact of population density can be seen in the Ruyigi region. In the two communes in this region with densities above the regional average, half the farmers cultivated an area of less than one hectare and only 12 per cent had more than 4 hectares; in the other three communes, the proportions were one-third and one-fifth respectively.

Social factors also influence the distribution of holdings. The religious factor has a significant effect in all three regions. Catholic farmers and those following the traditional religion had holdings of the same average size, but the holdings of the Protestants were larger. Among the former, 32 per cent had less than one hectare and 46 per cent more than two hectares; 24 per cent of the Protestants had less than one hectare and 63 per cent more than two hectares[6]. The variable selected to represent the sociologico-political factor was the frequency of the farmers' contacts with the district commissioner and the provincial governor. In two of the regions there was no correlation between this variable and size of holding, but in the third, Ruyigi, regular contact with the commissioner was associated with larger holdings: 39 per cent of these farmers had more than two hectares and 33 per cent less than one hectare. The figures for those who never had any such contacts were 24 per cent and 47 per cent.

2. Land use

It is useful here to distinguish between two variables: the non-utilisation rate and the fallow rate. The first is measured by the fraction of the land which, for one reason or another, is never cultivated; the second corresponds to that fraction which is temporarily not being cultivated in order to enable the soil to recover its fertility. Population density and size of holding obviously influence both these variables, as can be seen from Tables 2 and 3.

The utilisation rate was lower in the Bubanza region than in Ngozi and Ruyigi. In Bubanza (where the average size of holding was larger – 3.4 hectares against 2.7), the total area was cultivated in 65 per cent of the cases, compared with 73 per cent in the other regions. As for the differences between Ngozi and Ruyigi (only 11.6 per cent of the farmers used less than 70 per cent of their land in Ngozi as against 17.6 per cent in Ruyigi), these result from differences in population density: the land was more intensively used in Ngozi, which has the highest density, than in Ruyigi, the least densely populated of the three regions. In Bubanza, the reorganisation of the former peasant communities in the Mpanda and Mutimbuzi communes (with the four-hectare holdings reduced to 1.5 hectare and cotton replaced by rice) is reflected in more intensive land use than in the other communes. In fact, these other communes are the only ones which are representative of the different agrarian structure in Bubanza (i.e. much larger holdings than in Ngozi and Ruyigi); in these communes only 50 per cent of the holdings were fully cultivated, compared with 73 per cent in Ngozi and Ruyigi.

Population density and size of holding also tend to determine the fallow rate (see Table 3) since it is easier to leave land fallow where larger areas are available. It was in Bubanza that the practice was found to be most widespread (60 per cent of farmers, compared with only 14 per cent for Ngozi and 20 per cent for Ruyigi). Even here, it is necessary to make a distinction between Mpanda, where the fallow rate was 45 per cent, and the other Bubanza communes, where it was 70 per cent. The situation in this commune is the result of a reduction in the size of holdings as part of a rice project. This once more confirms the relationship

Table 2. Percentages of unutilised land (in relation to total land) by region and by commune

Regions and Communes	Percentages of respondents with proportions of unutilised land in the ranges:					Total	
	0	1-9	10-19	20-29	⩾30	%	Number of respondents
Bubanza	64.6	8.3	14.0	6.8	6.3	100	591
Rugombo	52.1	8.3	25.6	8.3	5.7	100	121
Buganda	48.1	13.2	17.8	10.1	10.8	100	129
Mpanda	76.7	4.8	7.9	5.7	4.9	100	227
Mutimbuzi	72.3	9.8	9.8	3.6	4.5	100	112
Other							2
Ngozi	73.8	8.2	3.7	2.7	11.6	100	512
Mwumba	86.1	6.3	1.3	3.8	2.5	100	79
Marangara	83.7	5.4	2.2	1.1	7.6	100	92
Kiremba	78.2	7.3	3.6	0.9	10.0	100	110
Ruhororo	62.4	6.8	6.0	5.1	19.7	100	117
Rango	64.9	14.0	4.4	2.6	14.1	100	114
Ruyigi	71.9	3.7	2.9	3.9	17.6	100	484
Ruyigi	77.9	3.2	1.1	4.2	13.6	100	95
Bweru	67.3	5.5	3.6	2.7	20.9	100	110
Musongati	78.2	1.0	1.0	3.0	16.8	100	101
Rutana	64.6	4.0	7.1	4.0	20.3	100	99
Kinyinya	72.2	5.1	1.3	6.3	15.1	100	79

Table 3. Percentages of land left fallow (in relation to total land), by region and communes

Regions and Communes	Percentages of respondents with proportions of land left fallow in the ranges:						Total	
	0	1-9	10-19	20-29	30-49	⩾50	%	Number of respondents
Bubanza	39.8	2.0	3.7	5.2	16.5	32.3	100	591
Rugombo	28.9	0.8	5.8	4.1	24.0	36.3	100	121
Buganda	30.2	4.7	5.4	5.4	20.2	34.2	100	129
Mpanda	55.1	1.3	1.8	5.7	9.7	26.4	100	227
Mutimbuzi	32.1	1.8	3.6	5.4	17.8	39.4	100	112
Other								2
Ngozi	86.1	5.5	2.1	1.6	2.6	2.0	100	512
Mwumba	89.9	3.8	2.5	1.3	2.5	–	100	79
Marangara	76.1	12.0	1.1	2.2	2.2	6.6	100	92
Kiremba	89.1	2.7	0.9	2.7	1.8	2.7	100	110
Ruhororo	86.3	5.1	2.6	0.9	4.3	0.9	100	117
Rango	88.6	4.4	3.5	0.9	1.8	0.9	100	114
Ruyigi	79.8	7.0	3.9	2.7	6.8	10.4	100	484
Ruyigi	75.8	7.4	7.4	1.1	1.1	7.5	100	95
Bweru	75.5	8.2	4.5	3.6	6.3	1.8	100	110
Musongati	85.1	5.9	2.0	3.0	4.0	–	100	101
Rutana	83.8	8.1	5.1	3.0	–	–	100	99
Kinyinya	78.5	5.1	0.0	2.5	7.6	6.4	100	79

between, on the one hand, the size of holding and the area per inhabitant and, on the other, the practice of leaving land fallow.

B. Proprietorial rights to land

The renting of land plays only a secondary role (only 10 per cent to 20 per cent of the farmers rented part of the land they cultivated) and the farmers either owned the major part through inheritance or purchase or had received it by allocation from the State.

The way in which land is transferred and acquired and the features of the laws of tenure require special attention. Allocation by the State has been important only in the regions where peasant communities have been created. As far as the study is concerned, this means Bubanza, where 53 per cent of the farmers were settled on land which, at least in part, had been allocated to them. In the other regions, this feature is insignificant: less than 10 per cent of the farmers had acquired even part of their land in this way.

The allocated land must be distinguished from the owned land because of the permanent obligations which go with it. In particular, the farmers on the allocated land are subject to more or less strict supervision of their activities by the authorities. The Burundi peasants, who are very attached to full and stable rights to property, are unhappy about the partial character of their title to the allocated land and in general prefer to enjoy full ownership rights to the land they farm. This is one explanation for the frequent abandonment of holdings in the peasant communities. Land allocation also has an effect on the choice of crops because the

Table 4. **Inherited land as a proportion of total available land by region**

Regions and Communes	Percentages of respondents with proportions of inherited land in the ranges:				Total	
	0	1-49	50-99	100	%	Number of respondents
Bubanza	87.5	4.2	3.4	4.9	100	591
Rugombo	83.5	3.3	3.3	9.9	100	121
Buganda	84.5	4.6	3.9	7.0	100	129
Mpanda	88.1	4.9	3.5	3.5	100	227
Mutimbuzi	93.7	3.6	2.7	0.0	100	112
Other						2
Ngozi	15.0	8.2	30.9	45.9	100	512
Mwumba	17.7	7.6	27.8	46.9	100	79
Marangara	16.3	9.8	29.3	44.6	100	92
Kiremba	20.9	7.3	29.1	42.7	100	110
Ruhororo	18.8	8.5	27.4	45.3	100	117
Rango	2.6	7.9	39.5	50.0	100	114
Ruyigi	15.1	7.6	17.4	59.9	100	484
Ruyigi	10.5	7.4	17.9	64.2	100	95
Bweru	9.1	14.6	21.8	54.5	100	110
Musongati	15.8	5.0	19.8	59.4	100	101
Rutana	16.2	3.0	13.1	67.7	100	99
Kinyinya	26.6	7.6	12.6	53.2	100	79
Total	42.0	6.6	16.5	34.9	100	1 587

26

State obliges the recipient to plant certain cash crops regardless of the return obtained by the farmer.

Inheritance is the principal way in which property is acquired, as shown in Table 4. Leaving aside Bubanza, where allocation predominates, it will be seen that 46 per cent of the farmers in Ngozi and 60 per cent in Ruyigi inherited the whole of the land they farm. In addition, 31 per cent and 17 per cent, respectively, inherited the major part of it. In all, 77 per cent in each of the regions inherited either the totality or more than 50 per cent of their holdings.

Even if it is less important than inheritance, land purchase deserves detailed examination because of the wide differences from one region to another and because of its influence on agrarian structure. The enquiry could not reach most of the farmers who had sold land, many of whom had left the countryside permanently to live in the towns. Thus, only 5 per cent of the farmers interviewed had sold land at one time or other in their lives. It is nevertheless interesting to note that it is in the most densely populated region, Ngozi, that sales were most frequent (9 per cent), whereas they were almost totally absent in Ruyigi (1 per cent). Furthermore, the plots sold were almost all small: half were less than 2 500 square metres. On the other hand, purchases of land were much more frequently reported by the farmers interviewed, as shown in Table 5.

Table 5.   **Percentages of farmers in each region having purchased land**

Regions	Purchased land as proportion of total cultivated land	
	<50 %	≥50 %
Bubanza	15.6	8.8
Ngozi	10.3	8.6
Ruyigi	5.8	6.6

This means that roughly a quarter of the farmers in the Bubanza region had purchased land and that for 8.8 per cent of them the purchases accounted for the major part of their holdings. At the other extreme, it was in Ruyigi that purchases had been least frequent: 12 per cent of the farmers. This is the only region where there is little commercial farming. Land purchase therefore appears to be linked to a desire to increase production for the market and in fact occurs most frequently in the Rusizi plain (Bubanza), the region most involved in the market economy because of the peasant communities, and least frequently in the region which is the least densely populated and operates a subsistence economy. In addition, landowners who do not farm their land are to be found only in the regions with commercial farming: 17 per cent of the buyers of the land sold by the farmers interviewed in Bubanza and 14 per cent in Ngozi were non-farmers, but the percentage was zero in Ruyigi. Obviously this cannot yet be considered a major phenomenon of concentration of land-ownership in the hands of a well-off urban middle class (traders, company-owners, officials), but the spread of commercial farming clearly attracts the investment of urban capital in land. Sensitivity on the part of the farmers to land purchase by non-farmers was particularly noticeable in Bubanza, where one-quarter of the purchasers, according to the people interviewed, were non-farmers, compared with 10 per cent in the other regions. In addition, the peasants see these purchases as the start of a process of concentration of land-ownership. This feeling was especially prevalent in Ngozi (42 per cent of the peasants interviewed) where land shortage is at its most acute because of the population density. It was less common in Ruyigi (27 per cent) and in those communes in Bubanza where the rice-growing peasant communities, with their small size of holding, have been set up. Here this opinion was held by only 17 per cent.

Whether land is inherited or purchased, the system of property rights is important. Any uncertainty or conflict over titles to land is likely to have an impact on productivity. The farmer will be less inclined to invest in soil improvement, or to change his production methods, if there is a risk that he will not himself benefit from the results because his title to the land concerned is contested. As a result, statistics on conflicts over inheritance, boundary disputes, and possession of written title deeds are useful in order to appreciate the guarantees enjoyed by a landowner.

In Bubanza, where the majority of farmers come from the interior of the country, inheritance conflicts, by definition, hardly exist, but many of the respondents referred to problems of the share-out of ancestral lands in their home regions. In fact, these conflicts had in many cases incited them to move to the peasant communities. In the other two regions, they seemed fairly frequent. According to traditional practice, the sharing-out of land is carried out within the family by the father or, if the share-out follows the father's death, by the member of the family designated to replace him; if no agreement is possible, the official authorities are asked to intervene, which is the case in about 6 per cent of the share-outs, according to the enquiry.

Disputes over field boundaries are more frequent, as is only to be expected because they oppose neighbours and not members of the same family. The exact boundaries were the subject of frequent disputes in Ngozi (34.5 per cent of those interviewed had been involved) and Ruyigi (18.8 per cent). There are several reasons for this: the shape of the fields is very irregular, the boundaries having been fixed by the present holders' ancestors according to their own customs and traditions; above all, the fields have never been measured and there is no cadastral survey. The high frequency of disputes in Ngozi stems from the population density. It is in the most heavily populated regions that the peasants give the greatest importance to each square metre of cultivable land. In Bubanza, disputes were fairly rare (7 per cent of respondents) because the lay-out and measurement of the land took place when the peasant communities were set up.

The majority of farmers have no title deeds. This was true for 80 per cent of respondents in four districts of Ngozi and Ruyigi. The proportion was only 65 per cent in Bubanza because this plain, organised into peasant communities in colonial times, is part of the modern sector and has a European legal system. It is in fact the region where the farmers attach most importance to the possession of a title deed (only 10 per cent considered it unimportant, against 27 per cent in the two other regions). These differences result from the precarious situation of a farmer in one of the peasant communities. He lives under constant threat of eviction from the land allocated to him by the authorities if he fails to observe the standards laid down for the crops and their yields or does not pay his dues to the regional development corporations. He is therefore much more anxious to hold a title deed than is a peasant living in the interior of the country and on land which has been handed down from generation to generation within the same family. In these cases, landownership is more stable and a formal title seems less essential.

C. *Renting of land and ground rent*

Although renting of land plays only a minor role, the variations from one region to another are nevertheless significant. It is least common in Ruyigi (only 10 per cent of the farmers rented any of the land they farmed and only 6.1 per cent rented more than 10 per cent) and in Ngozi (19 per cent and 11.6 per cent)[7]. Ngozi differs from Ruyigi because of the presence of commercial farming and the larger holdings. There is thus an incentive for the farmers to extend the areas they farm in order to produce more coffee.

Rents can take three forms: services, produce or money. The first two of these are typical of a traditional non-monetary economy where barter predominates, while money rents are the usual form in a market economy. The enquiry showed rent in the form of labour to be quite insignificant (only 6 per cent of respondents paid in this way), but both the other forms were frequently used, produce being predominant in Ruyigi (84 per cent) and money rents in the other two regions (more than 50 per cent, as against 30 per cent for produce rents). There is a simple explanation. It is difficult to pay money rents in a region with a subsistence economy such as Ruyigi. On the other hand, the spread of commercial farming in Bubanza and Ngozi enables most tenants to pay rent in this form.

The existence of commercial farming affects not only the form of payment, but also the amounts, as can be seen from Table 6.

Table 6. **Monetary value of land rent per hectare, by region**

FBU per hectare[1]	Bubanza		Ngozi		Ruyigi		Total	
	Number of respondents	%	Number of respondents	%	Number of respondents	%	Number of respondents	%
1 – 2 999	16	39.0	22	28.2	15	45.5	53	34.9
3 000 – 5 999	10	24.4	14	17.9	11	33.3	35	23.0
⩾6 000	15	36.6	42	53.9	7	21.2	64	42.1
Total	41	100.0	78	100.0	33	100.0	152	100.0

1. Payment in labour or in beer has been converted into money equivalent.

The rent per hectare exceeded 6 000 FBu in 37 per cent of cases in Bubanza and 54 per cent in Ngozi, as against 21 per cent in Ruyigi. These disparities result from differences in productivity per hectare. It is in the areas of subsistence farming that high rents are most rare, while they reach their maximum in the region where the main crop is coffee, the one most profitable for the farmer[8]. A relationship can in fact be seen, within each region, between the level of rents and the productivity obtained by the farmers. In Ngozi and Ruyigi, of those farmers paying rents of more than 4 000 FBu per hectare, 60 per cent had holdings with a production of over 20 000 FBu per hectare, while of those paying lower rents, only 35 per cent reached this level.

It is also noticeable that the area of land rented varies with the productivity of the holding. For the three regions together, the farmers who rented no land or less than 20 per cent often had low productivity (less than 10 000 FBu per hectare). At the other extreme, those who rented a large amount of land (more than 20 per cent of the total holding) often reached much higher levels, as seen in Table 7.

Among the farmers renting large amounts of land, high-productivity farmers (over 20 000 FBu) accounted for 43 per cent , and low-productivity farmers (less than 10 000 FBu) for 22 per cent. The corresponding percentages for farmers renting no land were almost the inverse (30 per cent high-productivity and 44 per cent low). This relationship appeared most

Table 7. **Productivity per hectare and proportion of rented land for all three regions**

Productivity per hectare in FBU[1]	Percentages of respondents with proportions of rented land in the ranges:			
	0	1-19	≥20	Total
0 – 9 999	43.9	46.5	21.9	43.0
10 000 – 19 999	26.3	20.4	35.4	26.3
≥20 000	29.8	33.1	42.7	30.7
Total	100.0	100.0	100.0	100.0

1. Including receipts from sale of cattle.

clearly in Ngozi where, among the large renters of land, only 11 per cent had low productivity but 61 per cent high productivity per hectare. In Bubanza, farmers reaching a high level of productivity rented less land because of the prices obtained for their products. Since the marketing of these crops, cotton and rice, is done entirely through para-statal organisations which impose very low prices, there is less incentive for the farmers to rent more land in order to raise production.

This special behaviour, therefore, does not invalidate the relation between renting of land and productivity of the holding. The peasant who rents a substantial proportion of his holding stands out from the rest by his enterprise and his capacity for management. He is often more open to technical progress, is a more efficient manager and acts as an entrepreneur in resorting to renting to achieve a better organisation of his activities and to increase his net income.

It remains to be seen whether the practice of renting land is in fact leading to the development of a non-farming landowner group for whom farm property is merely an investment. It turned out that such a group had in fact appeared in Bubanza, where 43 per cent of owners were non-farmers, according to the tenants. On the other hand, the proportion was insignificant (3 per cent) in the other regions, where the landlords are themselves farmers – and, most often, related to the tenant. The presence of commercial farming is not in itself a sufficient condition for the development of a non-farming landowner group, as shown by the fact that the situation was the same in Ngozi as in Ruyigi. Other factors are more important, in particular the proximity to the capital and thus to the traders, officials and others prepared to invest, the reason which explains the particular situation in Bubanza.

III. AGRICULTURAL PRODUCTION AND YIELDS

The information on yields derived from the study must first of all be compared with earlier estimates and also qualified, stressing the margin of error involved. There have in fact already been numerous studies of agricultural production in Burundi. One of these, by P.Leurquin, covered 1 210 farm households[9]. J. Woillet carried out a study of 5 000 plainland farmers as part of the IMBO project[10]. Another study, in the Ngozi area, by IRUSTAT[11], calculated the yields of both food and cash crops. Finally, SEDES made studies in several provinces (Ngozi, Gitega, Muyinga, Ruyigi and Mosso)[12] in preparing the national agricultural statistics needed by the Planning Ministry.

Table 8. Production of various food crops in Burundi

Type of food crop	Production in thousand tons, according to:			Cultivated area in thousand hectares, according to:			Yields in kg/hectare, according to:		
	The Plan[1] 1967	IMF[2] 1967	1970	The Plan[1] 1967	IMF[2] 1967	1970	The Plan[1] 1967	IMF[2] 1967	1970
Bananas	800.0	1 300.0	...	100.0	130.4	...	8 000	9 969	...
Cassava	200.0	931.9	1 576.1	66.7	158.0	255.5	2 999	5 898	6 171
Sweet potatoes	680.0	757.2	1 074.1	90.7	109.5	180.4	7 497	6 915	5 954
Beans	160.0	123.4	553.7	228.8	206.7	519.6	699	597	1 066
Sorghum	100.0	121.0	96.0	83.3	112.7	79.1	1 200	1 074	1 214
Maize	100.0	115.6	287.3	100.0	111.5	269.4	1 000	1 037	1 066
Peas	20.0	37.4	34.4	33.3	68.5	38.4	600	546	896
Rice	2.5	3.6	12.0	1.9	1.7	3.7	1 315	2 118	3 243

1. Ministère du Plan, République du Burundi, Plan quinquennal de Développement économique et social du Burundi 1968-1972, provisional version, p. 41.
2. Data supplied to the IMF by the Burundi authorities. See International Monetary Fund, Surveys of African Economies, Volume 5, Washington 1973, p. 228.
Note: The figures in the table show orders of magnitude only. The data in the 1968-1972 five-year plan differ substantially for certain crops from the figures provided by the Burundi authorities to the International Monetary Fund.

Table 8 sets out the global data estimated by extrapolation from this group of studies. The estimates vary considerably from one source to another for certain crops. This is attributable to the inevitable uncertainties involved in any extrapolation from local or regional results, leading to wide variations in estimated yields, especially for food crops. These differences have a number of causes; the physical conditions (soils, climate) may not be comparable in different regions; the investigatory techniques may be of different kinds; there may be difficulties in actually measuring the yields, all this resulting from the fact that most food crops are grown in association with others, the yields varying according to the type of grouping concerned. For example, the IRUSTAT study identified 250 types of grouping including 28 encountered very frequently.

In the course of the present study, up to 5 different groupings were found on a single holding. Yields were measured only for products cultivated in isolation, however. Measurement was a particularly complex task. In practice, the period of observation was limited to one year, but the harvesting of cassava, for example, is not performed in a single operation at the end of the season but is spread over the period between the eighth and the twenty-fourth months after planting. Moreover, a crop grown in isolation at the time of the enquiry could have been grown in association with others during the two previous growing seasons of the same farming year.

The results of these measurements for food crops are set out in Table 9. In spite of the complexities surrounding the gathering of information on the yields of these crops, it emerges clearly that the yields in Bubanza are far lower than those achieved in the other two regions. For example, for beans, the staple food in the diet of the farming families, the reported yields were three times higher in Ruyigi and four times higher in Ngozi than in the peasant communities of Bubanza, differences which cannot be explained by the physical conditions.

Table 9. **Yields of food crops grown in isolation, by region**

Type of food crop	Bubanza		Ngozi		Ruyigi		Total	
	kg/ha	No. of obs.	kg/ha	No.of obs.	kg/ha	No. of obs	kg/ha	No. of obs.
Cassava	5 644	80	6 523	127	4 270	141	5 389	354
Sweet potato	7 531	63	13 210	178	11 452	234	11 591	475
Beans	0 477	17	2 008	33	1 680	54	1 587	104
Bananas[1]	0 664	39	3 314	39	0 810	48	1 540	126
Sorghum	0 878	76	1 820	139	1 942	146	1 671	361
Maize	0 873	25	–	–	6 706	5	1 845	30
Rice	2 413	168	–	–	–	–	–	–

1. The production of bananas is measured in bunches per hectare and not kg (a bunch of bananas weighs 11.6 kg on average).

Table 10 shows both the yields for cash crops and the wide variations from one holding to another. In the case of coffee, 22 per cent of the holdings had yields which were at least three times higher than those of the least productive 48 per cent. In the case of rice, 32 per cent of the holdings produced more than 3 000 kg./hectare and 21 per cent less than 1 000 kg./hectare.

These estimates differ widely from those obtained from other sources. In this study, the estimate for coffee was 684 kg./hectare on average for Ngozi and 962 for Ruyigi, whereas the estimates by Capecchi[13] were 1 100 and 291, respectively. Similarly, the estimate for cotton

Table 10. Yields of coffee, cotton and rice

Region	Average production of coffee (kg/ha)	Percentages of respondents with coffee production in the ranges: (kg/ha)				Total	
		1-299	300-599	600-899	≥900	%	Number of respondents
Ngozi	684	51.6	19.7	9.0	19.7	100	370
Ruyigi	962	41.9	16.2	15.6	26.3	100	180
Total	823	48.2	18.8	11.3	21.7	100	550

Region	Average production of cotton (kg/ha)	Percentages of respondents with cotton production in the ranges: (kg/ha)			Total	
		1-199	200-399	≥400	%	Number of respondents
Bubanza	348	18.1	53.6	28.3	100	414

Region	Average production of rice (kg/ha)	Percentages of respondents with rice production in the ranges: (kg/ha)				Total	
		1-999	1000-1999	2000-2999	≥3000	%	Number of respondents
Bubanza	2 413	21.4	30.4	16.1	32.1	100	168

obtained from the present study was 350 kg./hectare, while according to the Burundi authorities yields range between 528 and 1 012 kg.[14].

The conversion into money value of the physical quantities produced is an indispensable condition for the calculation of the production of each holding because there is no mono-culture. The estimation of prices for each product, whether sold or consumed in the household, always raises difficult problems. The following description of the methodology is given so that the reader may fully appreciate the results given below, either for the value of production or for the farmers' income.

For the amounts consumed directly (taken as being the difference between the amounts harvested and the amounts sold) the price used was the average price per kilo actually paid to the farmers. This average price, derived from the data obtained in the study, represents the price at which the farmers in the three regions taken together actually sold the product. The prices observed on the principal Burundi markets[15] are in most cases higher than the prices obtained by the farmer. For example, the price of sweet potatoes varied from 2.8 to 7 FBu per kg in the markets (and 11.3 FBu at Bujumbara) whereas the average price paid to the farmer, according to our study, was 3 FBu. For sorghum, the price was 20 FBu according to the study, but ranged from 22.6 to 33.4 FBu in the markets. The real difference is even larger than these figures imply, because the study covered 1977, while the data on market prices are for 1975. In addition, in Burundi as in other countries, the prices paid by the farmers to tide themselves over between harvests or at times of shortage are two to three times higher than those they receive for their sales in normal conditions.

The prices for rice, cotton and coffee are fixed each year by the authorities. In the case of cotton and coffee, the prices are very close to those paid to the farmer. For rice, on the other hand, which is entirely consumed inside the country, there is sometimes a considerable gap between the official price and those found in the markets. In 1977, the price to the producer was 20 FBu but on the Bujumbara markets at the same moment it was over 60 FBu.

Using the prices obtained through the study for food crops[16] and official prices for the cash crops[17], the average value of production was calculated by holding and by region. No account was taken at this stage of other forms of income (wages obtained from outside activities, rents from land, etc.). The figures are for gross agricultural income and not net, because the cost of inputs was not deducted (wages paid to farm-workers, payment for rented land, depreciation of tools).

Table 11 shows the figures for average production per holding and its distribution.

It will be seen that the proceeds from sales of cattle have only an insignificant effect on the average value of production. On the other hand, cash crops have a decisive impact: production per holding was half as high again in Bubanza and Ngozi, where cash crops are grown, as in Ruyigi, where they are not. It is also worth noting that the average level of production was as high in Ngozi, where the holdings are small and there is no outside support, as in Bubanza, where the holdings are larger and there is help from the authorities. This apparently paradoxical result is caused by the official price policies. The farmers in Bubanza are obliged to sell their rice and cotton at prices well below those paid by the consumer. The State in effect imposes a levy which offsets, and even exceeds, the value of the aid it provides.

Table 11. **Average value of agricultural production by region and its distribution**

Region	Average value of agricultural production (FBU)		Percentages of respondents with annual production in the ranges: (FBU per year)						Total	
			1-19 999		20 000-39 999		⩾40 000		%	Number of respondents
	With cattle	Without cattle	With cattle	Without cattle	With cattle	Without cattle	With cattle	Without cattle		
Bubanza	29 682	28 181	42.0	43.7	34.4	34.5	23.6	21.8	100	591
Ngozi	29 092	28 727	35.7	36.1	45.9	46.1	18.4	17.8	100	512
Ruyigi	20 341	19 829	61.4	62.4	30.6	30.2	8.0	7.4	100	484
Total	26 628	25 794	45.9	46.9	36.9	36.9	17.2	16.2	100	1 587

The "with cattle" category includes respondents who do not own cattle. The difference between the total figures is therefore equal to total receipts from sales of cattle.

Because of the wide differences in average production in Ruyigi, very few holdings exceeded 40 000 FBu (less than 8 per cent) as against 18 per cent in Ngozi and 22 per cent in Bubanza. At the other extreme, the percentage of holdings with low production (less than 20 000 FBu per year) was higher in Ruyigi (62 per cent) than elsewhere. But it will be noticed that low-productivity holdings were more numerous in Bubanza (42 per cent), where the farmers have larger areas and use more advanced techniques (irrigation, fertilizer, drawn implements, tractors) than in Ngozi (36 per cent), with its traditional techniques.

In Bubanza and Ruyigi there is a similarity between the distribution patterns for production and size of holding (Table 1). For Ngozi, the dispersion for production is less than for size of holding (the ratio of the 40th percentile to the 80th is 0.5 for production and 0.25 for size of holding). A difference of such importance probably results from the exceptional efforts which the farmers with small holdings make to compensate their lack of land, a consideration which does not apply in the other two regions.

Average production has to be broken down by type of crop in order to have a better idea of the impact of cash crops on the total level of production.

The most important conclusion to be drawn from Table 12 is the absence of any negative effect of cash crops on food crops. As is well known, the expansion of cash crops is often perceived by the farmer as a threat to food production. Furthermore, the literature is full of denunciations of cash crops on these grounds, accusing them of responsibility for the food deficits now afflicting many regions of Africa. In fact, the study shows that cash crops have not reduced the production of food in the three regions. Ruyigi, where the majority of holdings grow no cash crops, is the region where food production is lowest. This difference is not due to the size of holding; if food production is calculated per active worker[18], the difference is even more marked (10 per cent less than Bubanza and 30 per cent less than Ngozi).

Table 12. **Production of food crops and cash crops, by region**

Average value in FBU

Region	Total production		Food crops	Cash crops (all farmers)	Cash crops (producers only)	Farms producing cash crops
	With cattle	Without cattle				
	(1)	(2)	(3)	(4)[1]	(5)[2]	(6)
Bubanza	29 682	28 181	19 416	8 765	11 074	86.6
Ngozi	29 092	28 727	25 074	3 653	4 828	75.2
Ruyigi	20 341	19 829	18 616	1 213	3 243	37.2
The three regions	26 628	25 794	21 017	4 777	7 526	67.9

1. (2) minus (3). The difference between columns (4) and (5) increases as the percentage of farmers growing cash crops falls.
2. Including rice.

The second point to be stressed is that food crops are still relatively important in all three regions. Even in Bubanza, where their share in production was lowest, it was still over two-thirds. This makes it impossible to talk of a cash crop specialisation inclining the farmer to reduce food production in order to increase sales and buy in part of his food needs. Whichever region is taken, average food production equalled or exceeded the level in holdings outside the market system. Cash crops therefore appear in general to be a supplement and not a substitute. The value of this supplement varied from 3 653 FBu (Ngozi) to 8 765 FBU (Bubanza), or from 15 to 45 per cent of the total value of food production. What is more significant is to take only those holdings actually growing cash crops (column 5 of Table 12), for which the figures were 4 828 FBu (Ngozi) and 11 074 FBu (Bubanza), or 19 and 57 per cent of total production, respectively. What this in fact shows is the special nature of the peasant communities in Bubanza, since on these holdings cash crops are well in excess of half the value of the food production, as compared with only one-fifth in Ngozi. This figure in fact substantially understates the potential increase in total production.

As has been mentioned, the authorities fix the buying price of rice at a very low level (one-third of the price in Bujumbura). Doubling the price of rice and slightly increasing the price of cotton would enable the Bubanza farmers to reach a production level of 20 000 FBU instead of the present 11 074 FBu. It would only take a change in the market-distorting policy concerning prices for cash crops to bring about a doubling of total production compared with the level achieved in a subsistence economy.

35

A more refined analysis, based on the distribution by holding and by crop, makes it easier to understand the differences between Ngozi and Bubanza. In certain holdings in Bubanza, the expansion of cash crops has indeed brought about a reduction in food crops. Whereas in Ruyigi's subsistence economy 29 per cent of the holdings had a level of food production of less than 10 000 FBu and in Ngozi the figure was 15 per cent, it rose to 43 per cent in the case of Bubanza. This shows that for a minority of holdings in this region there was in fact a risk of food dependency, with cash crops being substituted for food production. This was particularly the case for 12 per cent of holdings which were almost totally committed to specialisation, with food crops accounting for less than 10 per cent of total production. At the same time, it is in this region that, as might be expected, the percentage of holdings reporting cash crop production of over 10 000 FBu was highest (37 per cent, compared with only 11 per cent in Ngozi).

In Ngozi, the only cash crop produced is coffee; in Bubanza, there are two (cotton and rice), with rice the more widespread. Cotton is more widely grown in the plain (by two-thirds of the farmers) than rice (only 30 per cent). But the average value of cotton production is lower than for rice: cotton brings in gross receipts of 7 400 FBu for the grower; if rice is added, receipts are over 11 000 FBu per holding. The contributions of these two crops to agricultural income of the farmers are therefore different; rice accounts for more than one-fifth of the total value of agricultural production for 91.5 per cent of the holdings, compared with 58 per cent for cotton.

Among food crops, the pattern varies from place to place. Beans and bananas, the latter often used to make beer, predominate in Ruyigi, where they accounted for more than 30 per cent of food production on 58 per cent and 46 per cent of holdings, respectively. The same is true of Ngozi where the 30 per cent figure was exceeded on 39.8 per cent and 74.3 per cent of holdings. In contrast, cassava was the main food crop in Bubanza (42.7 per cent of total food production), the second crop being bananas (36.3 per cent). Maize, for its part, was by no means negligible in this region (18.6 per cent of production), although it was almost entirely absent in the others (less than 10 per cent of production in 96.2 per cent of holdings in Ngozi and 81.8 per cent in Ruyigi).

Since the average level of production per holding cannot be taken as an indicator of efficiency, it is useful to compare levels of production either per hectare or per active worker in order to appreciate the impact of cash crops in this regard.

Table 13 shows productivity per unit of land, on average and for individual crops. The difference between the productivity of available land and of cultivated land depends on the proportion of land that is uncultivated or left fallow (see Section II). The gap is much more marked in Bubanza than for the other two regions because the farmers there have holdings which are larger than the families are capable of working.

Productivity per hectare of cultivated land depends on the fertility of the soil, the amount of work put in, the techniques used and the prices of the different products. It was greatest in Ngozi, much higher than in Ruyigi (by 30 per cent) or Bubanza (by 74 per cent), with intensive farming making up for the shortage of land. It should also be stressed that even in Ruyigi, where cash crops are negligible and where the traditional techniques have been more widely preserved, productivity per hectare, at 23 000 FBu, was much higher than in Bubanza (17 300 FBu), where cash crops are most widespread and support and help from outside sources are a dominant feature. Not only was Bubanza the region where low-productivity holdings accounted for 37.6 per cent of the total number, against 33.5 per cent in Ruyigi, but, even more surprising, the percentage of high-productivity holdings (over 30 000 FBu per hectare) was much lower there than in Ruyigi (14 per cent as against 23.1 per cent) in spite of the presence of cash crops.

Table 13. **Production per hectare in the three regions**

	Bubanza	Ngozi	Ruyigi	Average for the three regions
Value of total production per hectare in FBU :				
Available land	11 829	26 031	19 290	18 684
Cultivated land	17 285	30 040	23 047	23 161
Percentages of holdings whose production per cultivated hectare is:				
<10 000 FBU	37.6	19.3	33.5	30.4
10 - 20 000 FBU	32.5	28.1	28.9	30.0
>20 000 FBU	29.9	52.6	37.6	39.6
Average value in FBU of production per hectare for:				
Cotton	12 223	–	–	12 223
Coffee	–	60 449	69 346	65 092
Food crops	15 475	31 985	23 655	23 236
Cassava	22 104	25 368	16 773	21 061
Beans	9 613	40 110	33 594	31 742
Sweet potatoes	22 569	38 605	34 564	34 462

The data on productivity per hectare for individual products reveal the gulf between the various cash crops. In Ngozi, coffee made it possible to reach 60 000 FBu per hectare, or twice the productivity for food crops, while cotton and rice had low yields by comparison – 12 200 FBu for cotton and 48 000 FBu for rice. The value of cotton production per hectare was less than for food crops and that of rice well below that of coffee. These differences are mainly the result of the prices imposed by the authorities.

For the food crops, also, tnere were sharp differences in productivity, by a factor of 2.3 to 1 within each region. Furthermore, the specialisation in Bubanza on cassava instead of beans, the dominant crop in the other two regions, accords with the differences in relative productivity for the two crops: in Bubanza cassava had a productivity of 22 104 FBu per hectare compared with 9 613 FBu for beans: in the other two regions the relationship was inversed (40 110 FBu for beans and 25 368 FBu for cassava in Ngozi and 33 594 FBu and 16 773 FBu, respectively, in Ruyigi). Overall, the highest average productivities per hectare were achieved with beans and sweet potatoes.

Among the cash crops, cotton is in a paradoxical situation. In theory, cash crops should have a higher productivity than food crops. This was true of coffee and rice, but the gross receipts per hectare of cotton were less than for food crops in the three regions (apart from beans in Bubanza, where they are not grown on any scale). In addition, the farmer is obliged to pay high fees to the regional development corporations in order to produce this crop, with the result that the net return per hectare is much lower than on food crops, on which no such fees are paid. In these conditions, the occasional opposition of the Bubanza farmers to planting cotton is hardly surprising. How can they have any incentive to do so when food crops, so easily sold on local markets or in the capital, bring in so much higher net returns? This abnormal situation for cotton explains the wide productivity gap between cash crops in Bubanza (cotton and rice) and Ngozi (coffee). But there was also a difference of two to one between these

37

regions in the productivity of food crops, which is surprising since these figures are not for productivity per hectare of available land (the average size of holding is much larger in Bubanza than in Ngozi and less of the available land is in fact cultivated) but per hectare actually cultivated. Thus the region with the most outside support was precisely the one where productivity was lowest (only half Ngozi's and two-thirds of Ruyigi's). It remains to be seen whether this shortfall applies also to productivity per active worker and is therefore to be taken as a sign of failure.

It is in fact interesting to calculate labour productivity in each region, by type of crop, but not in relation to the equipment used, since this is in all cases still highly rudimentary.

The favourable impact of cash crops is confirmed by Table 14, the labour productivity being 40 per cent higher in Ngozi and 53 per cent higher in Bubanza than in the traditional auto-subsistence economy of Ruyigi. This agrees with the smaller number of cases of extremely low productivity (less than 5 000 FBu) in the first two regions (21 per cent, as against 38.4 per cent for Ruyigi). In addition, labour productivity was higher in Bubanza than in Ngozi (by 9 per cent) although production per holding (excluding livestock) was slightly lower and, notably, productivity per hectare was little more than half as high. This is because the Bubanza farmers have more land per active worker than those of Ngozi. With equal land per worker, labour productivity would be lower. This is not, however, the result of a less efficient combination of inputs or of any particular failings on the part of the Bubanza farmers. As has already been stressed, they suffer from the policy of low prices for cotton and rice. An analysis taking all these factors into account would therefore have to weigh these results taking into account not only differences in land availability, numbers of workers and degree of outside support[19] but also price distortions. Only adjustments of this sort could enable one to weigh up the effectiveness of the outside support provided in Bubanza. It can merely be pointed out that the dispersion of productivity figures per active worker was greater there than in Ngozi, since in 25.4 per cent of the holdings productivity per active worker was less than 5 000 FBU, compared with 17.4 per cent in Ngozi, where average productivity was nevertheless lower.

Table 14. **Value of production per active worker, by region**

Region	Production per active worker[1] (FBU)	Percentages of holdings with production per active worker[1] of			Total %
		<5 000 FBU	5 to 9 999	≥10 000	
Bubanza	12 081	25.4	30.6	44.0	100
Ngozi	11 045	17.4	39.6	43.0	100
Ruyigi	7 876	38.4	36.0	25.6	100
Total	10 452	26.8	35.2	38.0	100

1. Including receipts from sales of cattle.

Comparison between Ngozi and Ruyigi, the two regions which have the least State intervention, reveals one major fact: in spite of the severe land shortage in Ngozi, coffee has led to a substantial increase in productivity per active worker. There is every reason to think that the gap between Ngozi and Ruyigi would be even greater if the latter region were to suffer from the same land shortage and have the same number of active workers per unit of cultivated area.

These figures show that, while labour productivity can be substantially increased by the introduction of cash crops, their precise impact remains uncertain as long as the distortions caused by the imposition of fixed prices persist. It is impossible to re-calculate the productivity figures simply by applying an alternative set of prices, because the farmers' behaviour (choice of crop, degree of attention and hence the resulting yields) itself depends on the relative prices for different crops. Different prices would therefore mean different yields, different production volumes and, hence, different levels of productivity per active worker.

IV. THE CHOICE OF CROP

As the study of agricultural production showed, most of the farmers in Bubanza and Ngozi grow several food and cash crops at the same time. Even Ruyigi is not solely an auto-subsistence economy; in fact, 37 per cent of the farmers in that region were shown to grow coffee and to derive a sizeable income from it (average production 3 243 FBu as against 4 820 FBu in Ngozi). It is therefore desirable to analyse the respective roles of these various crops and then explain the choices made by the farmers.

A. *Food crops*

Although food crops in all the regions account for the major part of total production, they do not occupy the majority of the land. In fact, in Bubanza 54 per cent of the farmers devoted less than 30 per cent of their land to them. The situation is very different in the other two regions, where the corresponding proportions were 87.3 per cent (Ngozi) and 94.8 per cent (Ruyigi). Even in Ngozi, where coffee has been introduced into most holdings, more than half the farmers reserved at least 90 per cent of the land for food crops. It is therefore only in Bubanza that there has been a marked reduction in food crops, as a result of the ease of marketing (and modern infrastructure), the nearness of the capital and also the strict controls governing the peasant communities. In fact, the difference is relative rather than absolute. Given the larger size of holding (70 per cent with more than 2 hectares, compared with 33 per cent in the other two regions) a much lower percentage corresponds to an absolute area of the same order, since the farmers in all three regions need roughly the same area to meet the subsistence needs of their own families.

It would be incorrect to equate food production with home consumption and to apply the term "degree of home consumption" to such ratios as: area devoted to food crops/total area or food production/total production. It is true that there is a certain degree of autonomy here, since the farmer has the choice between selling his food surplus or increasing his family's consumption, whereas he can only sell his cotton or his coffee. But food surpluses of precisely this kind do in fact exist and one therefore cannot assimilate food production to a subsistence economy and all production of cotton, coffee or rice to a market economy.

The marketing of food products is naturally carried out under very different conditions, with traders playing a minor role, as can be seen from Table 15.

In Ngozi and Ruyigi most of the trading takes place directly at the farmers' level, with officials or cooperatives almost entirely absent. These do, however, have a certain importance in Bubanza, because of the peasant communities and the development corporations. The development of a market economy linked to cotton and rice explains the greater activity of traders in this region.

Table 15. **Principal types of buyer of food products, by region**

Region	Farmer	Trader	Government official or cooperative	Total %
Bubanza	34.4	43.9	21.7	100
Ngozi	87.4	10.8	1.8	100
Ruyigi	73.4	22.8	3.8	100

B.   Cash crops and rice

In the thinking of the German, and later the Belgian, colonisers, there was never any question of developing cash crops before 1930. In fact, at the beginning of the century, with Burundi situated on the frontiers of the Congo and close to the Katanga mining region, it was hoped that the country would generate a food surplus for the urban populations of its neighbour. Some export trade did in fact develop, in spite of transport difficulties. The first aim of colonial policy was therefore simply the commercialisation of food products. After 1931, however, a programme was introduced for the expansion of coffee-growing, which had been started in 1904. Each farmer received 50 coffee-tree plants, which he had to plant on his best land, with regular manuring. By 1938, coffee covered 18 000 hectares and by 1959, 25 000. After independence there was a slight decline in this crop, but a vigorous expansion programme was then launched by the Government and the present area is 41 000 hectares. Originally, there was a close link between the expansion of coffee and fiscal policy – the farmer needed it to earn the money to pay the taxes which were first imposed in the same year of 1931.

Like coffee, cotton and rice were also imposed on the farmers. Any farmer settling on the new lands in Bubanza had to grow cotton on 20 per cent of the land he was allocated. Rice was also introduced by compulsion. When the rice-land peasant communities were first set up in 1969, each farming family received 1.25 hectares of cultivable land in the Imbo area[20]; of this, 0.5 hectares had to be reserved for cotton, 0.5 for rice and 0.25 for food crops. For both cotton and rice, however, many farmers refused to respect these norms and they had to be reduced. As a result, in the peasant communities, where each farmer should have planted 8 000 square metres of cotton, the enquiry showed that 45 per cent of the farmers in fact planted less than 7 500 square metres. For rice, the area had to be reduced to 0.25 hectares. The study also showed that many of the farmers in fact planted much less rice than the targets set: 66 per cent of the rice farmers devoted less than 0.5 hectares to it. There are several reasons for this behaviour. One is that the amount of land originally allotted to the families was too great for the labour available. Above all, there was a preference for the food crops which could be freely sold and so bring in a higher return than rice and cotton with their artificially low imposed prices[21].

The study also showed a large diversity in behaviour because some of the Bubanza farmers actually exceeded the norms. Table 16 sets out the distribution of holdings by area devoted to cotton or rice. (Those farmers who grow no cotton almost all grow rice.)

The data show a large degree of dispersion for the areas under cotton, since 14 per cent of the farmers devoted more than one hectare to it and 6.5 per cent less than 2 500 square metres. The same is true of rice: 20 per cent under 2 500 square metres and 12 per cent more than 7 500 square metres.

The situation of the coffee-growers is very different because they are free to grow whatever amounts they choose. Coffee is now grown in all regions of Burundi, but the extent

Table 16. **Distribution of holdings by area devoted to cotton or rice**

Bubanza

	‹2 500m²	2 500 à 4 999	5 000 à 7 499	7 500 à 9 999	≥10 000	Total %
Cotton	6.5	24.6	14	40.8	14	100
Rice	19.5	46.6	21.8	12.1		100

varies widely from one region to another. Hardly any is grown in Bubanza – only 3 per cent of respondents. In Ngozi, the situation is the inverse with almost all farmers (97 per cent) growing it. In Ruyigi, 51 per cent of the farmers interviewed had at least a few coffee trees. A plantation sector of the kind which is familiar in Kenya, Tanzania or Zaire hardly exists in Burundi. By contrast, coffee is grown on small holdings, often on tiny plots. In Ruyigi, for example, 45 per cent of coffee-planters had less than 500 square metres and 64.4 per cent less than 1 000 square metres. Even in Ngozi, which specialises in this crop, the corresponding proportions were 27.2 per cent and 53 per cent. Planted areas of more than 2 000 square metres accounted for only 26.6 per cent of cases in Ngozi and 17.8 per cent in Ruyigi. The situation was different in Bubanza, where there are very few producers but the areas are larger, with 61.9 per cent exceeding 2 000 square metres. Two factors are involved here. First, the land allotted to each farmer is larger; second, the farmers are more inclined to specialise, the share of crops sold for cash (cotton, rice, coffee, but also foodstuffs) being higher.

Nevertheless, the amount of land devoted to coffee remains relatively modest in all three regions. The proportion of farmers devoting more than 20 per cent of their cultivated land to coffee was around 20 per cent (20 per cent in Bubanza, 24.1 per cent in Ngozi, 17.4 per cent in Ruyigi). For most farmers, the proportion was less than 10 per cent (51.5 per cent of the coffee-planters in Ngozi and 65.3 per cent in Ruyigi). In spite of a value of production per hectare which is much higher than for cash or food crops, coffee remains in almost all cases a supplementary activity, even in Ngozi, where the value of food production was on average five times higher than that of coffee.

C. The choice of crop

The farmers are not free to choose between the various saleable crops (cash crops, rice and food crops in those cases where nearby markets exist). They are subjected to a number of constraints which lead them to adopt a crop pattern very different from the one which would result from an optimum allocation of factors of production in a market economy free from over-population.

These constraints are most obvious in Bubanza (norms imposed concerning areas planted to cotton or rice, dues payable to development corporations). In Ngozi, the shortage of land in relation to the rural population limits the expansion of cash crops, given the large area which has to be used for food crops to meet local needs. Finally, in both this region and Ruyigi the lack of infrastructure is a severe handicap for the marketing of crops, especially those with low prices per unit of weight.

Having indicated the reference data for the farmer's choice, namely the differences among the crops in productivity per unit of labour and of land, the next stage is to look at the impact on his behaviour of the various constraints and of the outside help and support he receives.

41

The two most obvious questions concerning crop choice are: do the cash crops increase labour productivity or land productivity? Cash crops (including rice) have been chosen for this part of the study, rather than marketed crops (including, in addition, saleable food crops) because of a conflict concerning these crops which has been smouldering for fifty years between the farmers and the colonial authorities (and now the Government). The former administration, like its successor, tried various non-economic methods of inciting the farmers to develop these crops instead of relying on price as the unique incentive. The question is whether the farmers' resistance stems from an appreciation of economic reality (if these crops increase productivity neither of land nor of labour) or from mentalities and attitudes which have nothing to do with this reasoning.

The impact of these crops on land productivity varies between regions; it is unfavourable in Bubanza but tends to be favourable in the other two regions, as can be seen from Table 17.

Table 17. **Productivity per hectare and importance of cash crops, by region**

Percentage of area devoted to cash crops[1]	Percentage of holdings with a value of production per hectare of: (FBU)			Total	
	<20 000	20 to 39 999	≥40 000	%	Number of respondents
Bubanza					
0	52.4	34.1	13.5	100	170
10 to 19	78.6	21.4	0.0	100	42
20 to 49	75.3	20.7	4.0	100	251
≥50	82.4	13.2	4.4	100	114
Ngozi					
1 to 9	57.0	25.8	17.2	100	256
10 to 19	28.1	40.5	31.4	100	121
20 to 49	40.2	34.0	25.8	100	97
Ruyigi					
0	63.1	24.2	12.7	100	236
1 to 9	66.0	23.5	10.5	100	162
10 to 19	52.3	34.1	13.6	100	44
20 to 49	48.4	22.6	29.0	100	31

1. Ranges containing fewer than 30 observations have been omitted because results from samples of this size are not significant.

In Ruyigi it is clear that these crops increase productivity per hectare: the proportion of holdings with low productivity per unit of land (less than 20 000 FBu) was shown to decline as the share of cash crops increases, while the reverse was true of the holdings where productivity per hectare was over 40 000 FBu. The association is less clear in Ngozi, where the low-productivity holdings accounted successively for 57 per cent, 28.1 per cent and 40.2 per cent as the share of cash crops increased from less than 10 per cent to 10-20 per cent and finally to 20-50 per cent. In contrast, the relationship was the reverse in Bubanza, where the proportion of low-productivity holdings increased with the share of cash crops. There is an easy explanation in the fact that this is the region where for two of the crops, cotton and rice, the authorities impose prices paid to the producer which are well below world prices, in the case of cotton, or prices on the Bujumbura market, in the case of rice. The farmers' resistance to these crops therefore seems to be based on rational economic arguments[22], just like their favourable attitude to coffee, which tends to increase the productivity of the land. The contrast between these two types of crop is confirmed by the figures for labour productivity in Table 18.

Table 18. **Labour productivity and cash crops**

Average value in FBU of production per day of work

Region	Coffee	Cotton	Rice
Bubanza	250	56	94
Ngozi	108		
Ruyigi	167		

Even if one excludes the coffee-planters in Bubanza because of the small size of the sample, there is an important difference to be seen between cotton and coffee, a day's work on the coffee plantations bringing the Ngozi farmer twice as much production as a day's work on cotton and the Ruyigi farmer three times as much. The difference was smaller in relation to rice, but still significant, with work on coffee bringing in 15 per cent more than rice in Ngozi and 78 per cent more in Ruyigi.

Distortions of this size clearly result from the constraints imposed on the farmers. Without them, it is likely that farmers would apportion their cultivated land to the various crops in such a way that the net labour productivity[23] of each would tend to equality. These constraints are of various types, some being inescapable, others being more flexible and more in the nature of incentives. They also stem from many different factors, not all of them stemming from the authorities, such as religion, property statutes, labour practices or the role of animals.

Ever since the first introduction of cash crops, the attitude of the Catholic Church has been far from neutral. The clergy encouraged[24] and continues to encourage these crops, as shown by a letter sent to the Government by the Burundi bishops on 19th May 1979, in which they make known the commitment of the Church to collaborate in the development of cash crops. The attitudes of the clergy are not, however, a determinant influence on the behaviour of the farmers. Catholic farmers do not adopt these crops more than pagan ones, the proportions of cultivated land being 15.4 per cent for the former and 16.3 per cent for the latter. Nevertheless, the religious factor has a certain impact, insofar as the Protestant ethic, conforming to the thesis of Max Weber, seems to foster enterpreneurship and saving. In the three regions examined, the Protestants devoted a considerably larger share of their cultivated land to cash crops (23.8 per cent).

The system of land-ownership and the use of outside labour also influence the choice of crops. The need to make payments for rented land or as wages forces the farmers to increase their money earnings and so to expand their cash crops. The proportion of cultivated land devoted to these crops was 15 per cent in the case of farmers owning all or part of the land, but 21 per cent for those farmers who rented all their land. The farmers who rent part of their land behave like the landowners because they mainly consist of farmers in Ngozi whose own holdings are too small to feed their families. Renting land therefore is not the sign of a decision to specialise in coffee, but rather of the constraint imposed by family needs. Those who rent all their land, on the other hand, are concentrated in Bubanza and have chosen to specialise.

They are also the ones who employ the most wage-earners: 55 per cent of the Bubanza farmers employed labour on a permanent or temporary basis, compared with 22 per cent in Ngozi and 20 per cent in Ruyigi. In all regions the farmers taking on outside labour devoted a larger share of their cultivated land to cash crops. The method of wage payment is also linked to the choice of crop. The higher the share of wages paid in cash, the higher the percentage of total area under cash crops. For the farmers paying wages entirely in kind the proportion was 4.1 per cent and for those paying entirely in cash, 20.3 per cent.

On the other hand, to the extent that ownership of cattle permits the accumulation of wealth and the acquisition of a certain power in rural societies, it also, in a way, relieves the need to introduce cash crops in order to increase money incomes. A cattle-owner can entrust his cows to other farmers and so create a dependency while still deriving an income. The study showed that cattle-owners did in fact devote a larger share of their land to food crops (91 per cent) than farmers owning none (82.9 per cent). However, this conclusion is somewhat flimsy, because there are only a small number of livestock farmers in the sample, being relatively rare in the three regions investigated.

Finally, the State influences the share of cash crops in a number of ways, one of the most effective being through the services it provides to farmers. In Burundi, these are supplied through the extension workers at farm level and by agronomists supervising the activities of the extension workers. The study showed that the farmers who were in contact with these extension workers and agronomists devoted much greater importance to cash crops than the others. Furthermore, it seems that the influence of the agronomists in this respect is greater than that of the extension workers.

Simultaneous examination of the effects of religion and extension shows the influence of the former. Taking each of the three groups (pagans, Catholics and Protestants) it turned out that the share of cash crops increased with the degree of external support for the pagans (and the Protestants) but declined for the Catholics. In addition, if one distinguished two groups of farmers – those who had little or no contact with the extension workers and those who saw them frequently – it became apparent that in the first group the Christian farmers grew more cash crops[25]. In the second group, on the other hand, the Catholics grew the least and the Protestants the most, with the pagans in between. In this way the religious factor is superimposed on the influence of extension and can even have a greater impact.

The operation of the extension service is not independent of the system of land tenure. It is both more widespread and more intensive in Bubanza, where most renters of land are concentrated. More than three-quarters of the farmers questioned in Bubanza had frequent contact with the extension workers, but the figure fell to 64 per cent in Ngozi and to 37 per cent in Ruyigi. As we have seen, cash crops are most widely grown where land is rented. These two factors combined provide the Bubanza farmers with the incentive to plant cash crops.

V. THE INPUTS

The level of farmers' expenditures on inputs is a good indicator of the stage reached in the evolution of agriculture. The level was lowest on the most traditional holdings, those where the farmer was the owner, where no cash crops were grown, where no outside labour was employed, where the equipment was rudimentary, where neither fertilizers nor selected seeds were used, etc. At the other extreme, the level increased with the proportion of rented land, with the use of hired labour, of machinery, of fertilizers – and with the development of cash crops, the only means of paying the additional expenses. The level of expenditure is therefore a measure of the stage of transition from traditional subsistence agriculture to a form of commercial agriculture linked to the market economy[26].

One conclusion to emerge from analysis of the inputs is the close connection between expenditure on inputs and the proportion of cash crops. The two main items of expenditure are wages and, in Bubanza, the payment of dues. Here, the farmers make a global payment to the regional development corporations for the various means of production provided by them, including the services of the extension workers and agronomists. This type of expense is non-existent in Ruyigi and very rare in Ngozi (where only 3.9 per cent of the farmers paid amounts not exceeding 4 000 FBu). In contrast, 15.2 per cent of the farmers in Bubanza paid dues of more than 4 000 FBu (corresponding to a normal level of payment, since the total for the various services provided is 6 000 FBu) and 21.2 per cent paid less than 4 000 FBu. The dues are only a trifle for the rich farmers, but they can be a relatively heavy burden for the others, some of whom find it impossible to pay the totality in drought years.

Analysis of farmers' monetary expenditure on inputs shows a sharp split between the Rusizi plain and the interior of the country, due to a higher degree of monetisation of agriculture and larger holdings in the plain.

Table 19 clearly shows the difference between agriculture in the Rusizi plain, highly integrated into the market, and the traditional subsistence agriculture of the interior. In the most modern sector of the Burundi economy, the farmers spending less than 1 000 FBu annually on inputs in the broadest sense are relatively three times less numerous than in the interior (25 per cent against 78.7 per cent). Conversely, relatively many more farmers in the plain spend more than this amount: in Bubanza, 51.3 per cent of respondents devoted 3 000 FBu or more annually to this form of expenditure, compared with only 6.5 per cent in the interior.

Table 19. **Annual monetary expenditure by households on production inputs, by region**

Region	Percentages of households with expenditure on inputs in the following ranges:[1] (FBU)				Total	
	0-999	1 000-1 999	2 000-2 999	⩾3 000	%	Number of respondents
Bubanza	25.0	13.4	10.3	51.3	100	591
Ngozi + Ruyigi	78.7	12.1	2.7	6.5	100	996
Total	58.8	12.6	5.5	23.1	100	1 587

1. Expenditure on livestock, tools, seeds, various charges (insecticides, irrigation, fertilizers, draught animals, etc.) and money wages paid to outside workers.

After this presentation of the global data on the farmers' payments for inputs, the next stage is to examine the role played in production by each type of input, whether or not the subject of an actual payment.

A. Labour

The quantity of labour which the farming families devote to agricultural production can be measured by the number of full-time units involved, adult or child, member of the family or employed worker. Children were counted as half a unit. Labourers or members of the family working part-time were converted to a full-time basis on the basis of a 300-day working year. Table 20 shows the distribution of holdings by number of full-time units of labour.

Table 20. **Labour input: distribution of holdings by number of full-time workers**

Region	≤1	2	3	4	≥5	Total
Bubanza	19.3	42.6	20.6	11.5	6	100
Ngozi	5.9	42.6	23.6	19.1	8.8	100
Ruyigi	9.1	43.8	20.2	16.7	10.2	100
Total	11.8	43	21.5	15.7	8	100

The Bubanza region used by far the least labour, with nearly 20 per cent of the holdings employing only one person or less full-time, compared with 5.9 per cent and 9.1 per cent in the other two regions. It is in the two interior regions, also, that the highest proportions of holdings with a large labour input (4 or more units) were found: 27.9 per cent and 26.9 per cent compared with 17.5 per cent in Bubanza. These differences are partly explained by the fact that in the cotton- and rice-growing peasant communities many of the farmers are young and only recently installed, have not yet married, or have only recently done so, and so have no children or only very young ones living with them. In addition, farmers often leave this region within only a few years of arrival, with the result that the population in these peasant communities is much less stable than in the interior of the country, where the large traditional patriarchal families are still common.

These figures reflect only part of the truth, however, because the smaller holdings inevitably under-use the available manpower when this exceeds two units, which is often the case in Ngozi. To have a better idea of the labour actually devoted to production, taking account of the hidden unemployment resulting from over-population, and to arrive at a better estimate of the possibilities of achieving an increase in production by using more labour, it is useful to calculate labour input per hectare of land available or of cultivated land.

Labour input per hectare was calculated in two ways, one measuring the theoretical intensity, the other effective intensity. The first assumes that each adult works 300 days a year; the second takes into account the number of days actually devoted to each crop, including harvesting. The trends which emerge at regional levels were the same for both indicators, as shown in Table 21.

A sharp difference will be noted between Bubanza and the regions of the interior. In the peasant communities, labour intensity was much lower, the number of days actually worked being less than 300 a year in more than half of the holdings in Bubanza, compared with 36.1 per cent of holdings in Ngozi and 32.9 per cent in Ruyigi. Conversely, figures of 900 days or more were the exception in Bubanza: 4.3 per cent compared with 20.5 per cent and 26.8 per cent in the other two regions, where labour intensity was nearly identical. These differences have nothing to do with the nature of the crops in Bubanza. Taking the same crop, coffee, the proportion of holdings devoting less than 300 days of labour to it was 75 per cent in Bubanza compared with 34.1 per cent in Ngozi and 43.9 per cent in Ruyigi. Food crops are grown in all three regions, yet the figure of 600 days was exceeded in only 14.8 per cent of the holdings in Bubanza as against 37.2 per cent in Ngozi and 43.9 per cent in Ruyigi. The special situation in Bubanza is therefore not the result of the crop pattern, but rather, it would seem, of the combination of larger sizes of holding and smaller families.

46

Table 21. **Labour input per hectare**

Region / Labour intensity (theoretical or effective)	Percentages of amatongo with days of labour input per hectare of land available or under cultivation of:								Total	
	Land under cultivation				Land available				%	Number of respondents
	0-299	300-599	600-899	≥900	0-299	300-599	600-899	≥900		
Bubanza										
Theoretical	28.8	38.4	17.8	15.0	62.6	20.3	7.6	8.5	100	
Effective	49.6	38.1	8.0	4.3	75.0	19.5	3.5	2.0	100	591
Ngozi										
Theoretical	20.5	21.7	19.3	38.5	24.8	23.8	18.8	32.6	100	
Effective	36.1	30.5	12.9	20.5	42.2	28.9	11.5	17.4	100	512
Ruyigi										
Theoretical	21.9	17.1	18.2	42.8	28.1	19.2	15.7	37.0	100	
Effective	32.9	25.4	14.9	26.8	41.1	24.4	13.4	21.1	100	484
All three regions										
Theoretical	24.0	26.5	18.4	31.1	39.9	21.1	13.7	25.3	100	
Effective	40.1	31.8	11.7	16.4	54.1	24.0	9.1	12.8	100	1 587

Since the conditions under which production takes place in the three regions are relatively homogeneous, it is possible to proceed to analyse the relationships between labour input per hectare and production per hectare.

Table 22 clearly shows that the productivity of land is a function of the amount of labour per hectare: the greater the labour intensity, the higher the productivity of the land. This conclusion holds for all three regions. This implies that any additional unit of labour applied to the land results in some increase in the value of production per hectare of cultivated land. In practice, both in Bubanza and in the interior, the proportion of holdings where productivity is low (less than 20 000 FBu) diminishes as labour intensity increases, the reverse being true for the proportion of holdings with productivity of over 40 000 FBu per hectare. Ngozi is the region where this relationship comes out most clearly, with the percentages of holdings with low productivity (less than 20 000 FBu) going from 81.1 per cent to 43.6 percent, 16.7 per cent and 13.3 per cent as labour intensity rises from less than 300 days of work per hectare to 300-599, 600-899 and 900 days or more, respectively. In the same region, in the cases of high productivity (≥ 40 000 FBu), the percentages rise from 3.8 per cent to 17.3 per cent, 30.3 per cent and 57.2 per cent as labour intensity per hectare rises.

At the same time, there are still reserves of productivity to be exploited, in terms of cultivated land. There is further potential in the fact that only part of the available land is actually cultivated. The existence of these reserves can be inferred by comparing the intensity of labour input per unit of cultivated area with that per unit of available land. In principle, the greater the difference, the greater the potential for additional production through increases in labour input. Thus, in Bubanza, 28.8 per cent of the holdings applied less than 300 days of work to each hectare of cultivated land, but the proportion was 62.6 per cent if related to the total land available. The theoretical increase in labour input is therefore of the order of 30 per cent. In Ngozi and Ruyigi, the theoretical possibilities of increasing labour intensity are much smaller, the differences being only 4 per cent and 6 per cent.

Table 22. **Labour input and production per hectare, by region**

Effective labour intensity[1] (number of days per hectare)	Percentages of respondents with values of production per hectare in the range: (FBU)			Total	
	1-19 999	20 000-39 999	⩾40 000	%	Number of respondents
Bubanza					
Total	70.0	23.4	6.6	100	591
0-299	83.3	14.3	2.4	100	293
300-599	64.9	29.3	5.8	100	225
600-899	36.2	42.5	21.3	100	47
⩾900	26.9	38.5	34.6	100	26
Ngozi					
Total	47.4	30.3	22.3	100	512
0-299	81.1	15.1	3.8	100	185
300-599	43.6	39.1	17.3	100	156
600-899	16.7	53.0	30.3	100	66
⩾900	13.3	29.5	57.2	100	105
Ruyigi					
Total	62.4	24.6	13.0	100	484
0-299	93.1	6.3	0.6	100	159
300-599	70.7	22.0	7.3	100	123
600-899	48.6	41.7	9.7	100	72
⩾900	24.6	40.0	35.4	100	130
Total	60.4	26.0	13.6	100	1 587

1. The effective labour intensity is based on indications from the respondents concerning the number of days actually spent in agricultural work, both by members of the household and outsiders. The number of days worked was recorded separately for each type of agricultural work, for both food crops and cash crops.

B. Land

The study of agrarian structure in Section II gave a detailed picture of the amounts of land used in production. The following remarks are therefore confined to an analysis of the productivity of land as a function of the size of holding. In theory, it should increase with the size of holding, since one normally assumes that the "medium-sized" farmer – there are no really large holdings in the three regions – have easier access to farm credit and to modern techniques (fertilizer, selected seeds, tools of advanced design, etc.) than the "small" farmer. What emerges from the study is quite the opposite, as shown in Table 23.

Whichever region is taken, the tendency is the same: the smaller the holding, the higher the productivity per unit of land. This tendency was even more marked in the interior of the country than in Bubanza: taking the holdings of less than half a hectare, the highest recorded level of productivity (30 000 FBu per hectare) was achieved in 70.4 per cent of these holdings in Ngozi, 56.8 per cent in Ruyigi and only 47.4 per cent in Bubanza. This result is due to the low level of techniques applied. With hoes, machetes and pruning knives as the main tools, it becomes very difficult for a household to achieve a reasonable degree of exploitation of all its land once the area involved exceeds the family's strictly limited working capability[27].

Table 23. **Size of holding and productivity per hectare of available land**

Available land (hectares) by region	Percentages of respondents with values of production per hectare in the range: (FBU)				Total	
	1-9 999	10 000-19 999	20 000-29 999	≥30 000	%	Number of respondents
Bubanza	59.2	23.7	9.0	8.1	100	591
0-0.49	26.3	10.5	15.8	47.4	100	19
0.50-0.99	17.5	27.5	25.0	30.0	100	80
1.00-1.99	41.5	29.9	14.3	14.3	100	77
2.00-3.99	64.5	26.4	7.6	1.5	100	197
≥4.00	78.9	18.8	1.8	0.5	100	218
Ngozi	26.2	27.3	18.0	28.5	100	512
0-0.49	8.6	4.9	16.1	70.4	100	81
0.50-0.99	6.7	23.6	18.5	51.3	100	119
1.00-1.99	11.5	35.0	36.4	17.1	100	140
2.00-3.99	41.0	51.6	4.2	3.2	100	95
≥4.00	83.1	13.0	2.6	1.3	100	77
Ruyigi	41.0	28.3	12.6	18.1	100	485
0-0.49	3.2	18.9	21.1	56.8	100	95
0.50-0.99	16.7	37.3	23.5	22.5	100	102
1.00-1.99	35.7	45.3	10.3	8.7	100	126
2.00-3.99	68.0	28.0	4.0	0.0	100	75
≥4.00	95.4	3.4	1.2	0.0	100	87
Total	43.0	26.3	13.0	17.7	100	1 588
0-0.49	7.7	12.3	18.5	61.5	100	195
0.50-0.99	13.0	29.2	21.9	35.9	100	301
1.00-1.99	27.1	37.6	21.9	13.4	100	343
2.00-3.99	59.1	33.3	6.0	1.6	100	367
≥4.00	83.5	14.2	1.8	0.5	100	382

C. Livestock

The term "livestock" comprises large animals (cattle) and small (goats, sheep, pigs, and also poultry). It can be a direct means of production (milk or meat for sale or home consumption) or an indirect one (manure for agricultural use) or it can have a social value, since cattle give their owner prestige and even a certain power (even if this aspect has declined in today's society) and are of definite importance in matrimonial affairs because they provide the basis for the dowry. The replies to the question "What does the cow mean to you?" showed, however, that social values play only a minor role, being mentioned by only 3.7 per cent of the farmers. On the other hand, 36.7 per cent referred to family consumption of milk and meat, 29.1 per cent to the sale possibilities and 30.5 per cent to the use of manure on the farm.

Livestock activities were more widespread in Ruyigi than in the other two regions, with 31.4 per cent of holdings having livestock worth more than 30 000 FBu, compared with 20.7 per cent for Bubanza and 13.8 per cent for Ngozi. Taking just the large animals, which are owned by only a minority of farmers (384 respondents out of 1 027), these are heavily concentrated in Bubanza, where 45.6 per cent of livestock-owners reported a total value of over 40 000 FBu, as against 11.2 per cent in Ngozi and 18.4 per cent in Ruyigi. The same differences between the regions were found in receipts from the sale of cattle (see Table 24).

For the large animals, 70.5 per cent of the livestock-producers in Bubanza achieved sales of over 10 000 FBu, compared with 22.3 per cent in Ngozi and 31.6 per cent in Ruyigi. There was the same advantage in favour of Bubanza with respect to sales of small animals, with 31.2 per cent exceeding 2 000 FBu, compared with 10 per cent in the regions of the interior, or of livestock of all sizes (roughly a quarter of the Bubanza respondents recording sales of over 5 000 FBu as against 7 per cent in Ngozi and 14 per cent in Ruyigi). Sales of small animals were much more common than of cattle. In the three regions taken together, one farmer in five sold small animals and/or poultry during the period of observation, while sales of cattle were recorded by only one respondent in 25[28].

It should theoretically be possible to increase the productivity of labour or land if the farmer systematically applies natural fertilizers (manure, compost) or chemical ones to feed the land or uses oxen to draw ploughs or harrows to work it. This last practice is in fact rarely used, being found almost only in Bubanza.

Table 24.   **Receipts from sales of livestock, by region**

Region and type of livestock	Percentages of respondents with sales of livestock in the range: (FBU)				%	Number of respondents having sold livestock
	≥2 000	1-4 999	5 000-9 999	≥10 000		
Bubanza						
Large and small livestock and poultry		75.5	7.7	16.8	100	155
Large livestock only		3.0	26.5	70.5	100	34
(small livestock and poultry)	(31.2)					(141)
Ngozi						
Large and small livestock and poultry		92.7	4.2	3.1	100	96
Large livestock only		44.4	33.3	22.3	100	9
(small livestock and poultry)	(12.5)					(84)
Ruyigi						
Large and small livestock and poultry		85.3	9.2	5.4	100	109
Large livestock only		31.6	36.8	31.6	100	19
(small livestock and poultry)	(8.3)					(41)
Total						
Large and small livestock and poultry		83.0	7.2	9.7	100	360
Large livestock only		17.6	30.7	51.6	100	62
(small livestock and poultry)	(19.4)					(325)

D.   Agricultural equipment

The only items of agricultural equipment owned by the farmers are simple tools like axes, pruning-hooks and hoes, the latter being the most important (either of local origin or imported from England). Modern equipment like agricultural machinery or tractors are seen mainly in the cotton- and rice-growing peasant communities in Bubanza. These are not owned by the farmers but by the regional development corporations. Mechanisation of this kind has to be justified, since Burundi is characterised by a shortage of land and an abundance of labour.

Table 25 shows that the hoe, the axe and the pruning-hook are the only tools in widespread use on all holdings. The other assets (baskets, sacks, grain stores, beer-troughs) are used more for storage and transport than for production. The farmers in Bubanza own more than the others because commercial marketing of agricultural produce is more developed in this region.

Table 25.   **Farm implements and length of use, by region**

Type of implement	Average number of implements per respondent household			Number of observations			Average number of months of use		
	Bubanza	Ngozi	Ruyigi	Bubanza	Ngozi	Ruyigi	Bubanza	Ngozi	Ruyigi
Hoe	4.1	3.3	3.1	590	511	483	37.9	43.4	39.8
Machete	1.4	1.5	1.3	477	339	263	71.1	78.8	72.8
Pruning knife	1.2	1.4	2.0	186	278	432	53.3	69.7	45.7
Basket	3.2	2.8	2.5	515	471	444	17.6	20.8	16.0
Salt sack (25 kg)	2.6	1.7	1.8	132	224	267	23.9	35.5	20.0
Sack (50 kg)	2.5	1.6	1.8	93	210	96	32.9	40.2	30.3
Sack (100 kg)	3.4	1.8	1.5	254	40	31	30.2	40.2	32.0
Grain store	2.8	1.5	1.6	16	79	89	44.8	52.9	44.4
Beer-trough	1.1	1.2	1.1	172	339	284	126.4	132.8	100.5
Churn	1.1	1.1	1.1	63	81	158	124.1	136.9	102.0
Milk pot	2.4	4.3	2.5	52	80	149	79.9	106.2	90.3
Hive	3.4	2.8	3.5	15	79	34	52.7	40.0	40.7

In contrast, the non-traditional tools from abroad are, with one or two exceptions, rarely used. It is true that about 80 per cent of the farmers reported owning an axe, but picks, rakes, wheelbarrows, forks and sickles were rarely found (on average on 2 to 3 per cent of holdings). Mattocks were found in any numbers only in Bubanza, where 31 per cent of the farmers owned one as against 4 per cent elsewhere. As for the tractors belonging to the development corporations, the only farmers to use them were a minority in Bubanza (21.8 per cent) who ploughed and otherwise prepared their fields with them.

The average value of these tools was small, varying from 1 345 FBu in Ruyigi to 1 504 FBu in Bubanza. Ownership was fairly evenly distributed, with 83.5 per cent of holdings in Ngozi and 85.1 per cent in Ruyigi reporting values between 500 and 2 000 FBu. Ownership was somewhat more concentrated in Bubanza, where the 2 000 FBu figure was exceeded in 23.6 per cent of cases, compared with 15.5 per cent in Ngozi and 12.2 per cent in Ruyigi. But since the average size of holding is much larger in Bubanza (3 871 square metres as against 2 945 square metres in Ngozi and 2 911 square metres in Ruyigi), the value of equipment per hectare of cultivated land was much lower (984 FBu as against 1 782 FBu in Ngozi and 1 853 FBu in Ruyigi). On the other hand, the ratio of capital (equipment) to labour was much higher there, given the lower amount of labour per hectare (see Table 20). The average value of tools per worker in Bubanza was 737 FBu, compared with 595 FBu in Ngozi and 520 FBu in Ruyigi. Bubanza had just as many under-equipped farmers (13.7 per cent reported less than 300 FBu, compared with 7.6 per cent and 13.4 per cent in the other two regions) but the proportion of farmers with equipment worth more than 900 FBu was higher (15.9 per cent against 6.4 per cent). It would seem, therefore, that the expansion of cash crops is

51

accompanied by an increase in the capital/labour ratio resulting from an effort to build up equipment on the part of some, but not all, of the farmers.

The study shows (Table 26) that buying tools is an extremely profitable investment for the farmer. For example, a Ngozi farmer who spent 500 FBu per hectare (going from the 500/1 000 FBu range to 1 000/1 500 FBu) could expect to increase production per hectare by about 4 000 FBu, or eight times his investment. In each region, there was a clear relationship between the value of equipment and production per hectare, the under-equipped farmers (with less than 500 FBu per hectare) being those with the least productive holdings – less than 20 000 FBu in all cases in Ngozi and Ruyigi and in 94.8 per cent in Bubanza. At the other end of the scale, those with values of over 1 500 FBu per hectare obtained the highest productivity. This comes out most strongly in Ngozi, where 47.6 per cent of this group reached production levels of over 40 000 FBu per hectare, as against 5.1 per cent and 10.3 per cent for farmers in the 500-1 000 and 1 000-1500 FBu ranges. It emerges from these figures that there are in each region considerable untapped reserves of productivity, in the sense that productivity per hectare increases sharply with value of equipment per hectare. For example, in Ngozi land productivity almost doubled as equipment rose from 750 FBu to 1 800 FBu per hectare. It would take only relatively modest investment in improved traditional tools, produced in Burundi, to achieve a substantial increase in the productivity of land, and so in agricultural production and in the standard of living.

Table 26. **Value of farm implements per hectare
and productivity per hectare of cultivated land, by region**

Value of implements in FBU per hectare of cultivated land, by region	Percentages of respondents with values of production per hectare in the range: (FBU)			Total	
	0-19 999	20 000-39 999	≥40 000	%	Number of respondents
Bubanza	70.0	23.4	6.6	100	591
0- 499	94.8	5.2	0.0	100	135
500- 999	76.3	22.0	1.7	100	236
1 000-1 499	56.1	35.5	8.6	100	139
≥1 500	34.6	37.0	28.4	100	81
Ngozi	47.5	30.3	22.2	100	512
0- 499	100.9	0.0	0.0	100	92
500- 999	69.2	25.7	5.1	100	117
1 000-1 499	46.4	43.3	10.3	100	97
≥1 500	12.1	40.3	47.6	100	206
Ruyigi	62.4	24.6	13.0	100	484
0- 499	100.0	0.0	0.0	100	105
500- 999	84.5	12.4	3.1	100	97
1 000-1 499	65.4	33.3	1.3	100	78
≥1 500	31.4	39.7	28.9	100	204

E. Production techniques

Improved techniques, together with equipment, are among the most effective ways of increasing the productivity of labour and land. The techniques most widely used are the manuring of fields, selected seeds, crop rotation, fallowing and anti-erosion practices. These techniques were more commonly found in the regions of the interior than in Bubanza where, partly as a result of colonisation, change has gone deepest.

The study concerned itself only with whether or not different types of fertilizer (natural[29], chemical or mixed) were used and not with the particular composition of the chemical fertilizer or the precise amounts. Fertilizer use was broken down by type of crop. The first result concerned the extent of fertilizer use. It turned out that 80 per cent of the Ruyigi farmers and 87.5 per cent of the Ngozi farmers used it, but the figure was less than 29 per cent in Bubanza. Even in the district of Mpanda, where the SRDI rice project is situated and where there is considerable external support, only half the farmers used fertilizer. The high percentage in Ngozi would seem to result from the dense population and the shortage of land which force the farmers to keep up the fertility of the soil in this way, because fallowing is hardly possible.

The types of fertilizer used by farmers were different in the three regions. In Bubanza, two-thirds of the fertilizer-using farmers relied on imported chemical products and even in Mpanda this was the only type used. On the other hand, natural fertilizer was the only type used in Ruyigi and predominated in Ngozi, where three-quarters of the user farmers applied nothing else and one-quarter combined it with chemical fertilizer.

Productivity per hectare might be expected to increase with fertilizer use, but this was not borne out by the facts. It is true that in Bubanza land productivity was closely related to it, with production per hectare exceeding 40 000 FBu for 13 per cent of fertilizer-users, compared with 4.1 per cent of non-users, and was in the 20 000 to 40 000 FBu range for 37.3 per cent of users, compared with 17.5 per cent of non-users. In Ngozi, however, the productivity of land was nearly the same for the two groups, and in Ruyigi the reverse was true, with proportionately more users than non-users in the low-productivity group (less than 20 000 FBu per hectare). This may be caused by the abundance of land in this region, giving the possibility of opening up virgin land when the cultivated land becomes exhausted.

The effects on productivity of land are not the same for natural and chemical fertilizers. In Bubanza, better results were obtained with chemical fertilizers. In Ngozi, on the other hand, where these were used only in combination with natural fertilizers, farmers using only natural fertilizers achieved higher productivity than those using both types.

The most ancient and the most widespread technique in Africa for enabling the soil to regain its natural fertility is the method known as "slash and burn". This technique is impracticable in Burundi because of high population density – along with Rwanda, the highest in the whole of Africa. The farmer is therefore forced to resort to fallowing and/or fertilizer to maintain fertility. In Bubanza three-quarters of the farmers who used fertilizers did no fallowing, while 62 per cent of the non-users left 30 per cent or more of their land fallow. In Ngozi, on the other hand, there was no connection between fallowing and use of fertilizer. Finally, in Ruyigi, the percentage of fertilizer-users was higher among those who also used fallowing. In this case, the combined application of the two techniques partly explains the high levels of productivity achieved by a small group of farmers in this region[30].

Although selected seeds are taken separately here, this technique must always in fact be seen in relation to a whole set of techniques (fallowing, fertilizer, anti-erosion practices) with which they are inextricably linked. In each region, the use of selected seeds was equally widespread, with about half the farmers using them. Studies in other developing countries indicate that it is normally the rich farmers who sow selected seeds, but the study showed that in Burundi the percentage of holdings using selected seeds remained practically constant, irrespective of the size of the holding, except for those of over 4 hectares where the percentage was well above the average (by 4 to 10 points).

In the regions of the interior, the process of seed selection was carried out only by the farmers. In Bubanza, on the other hand, the modern selection techniques promoted by the extension workers and agronomists led to 18.1 per cent of the farmers obtaining their seeds from them and 5.3 per cent from a dealer. For cash crops, preparation of seeds in specialised centres was the general rule, while for food crops this technique was left to the initiative of the farmers. The degree of use varied with the crop. It was lowest for sweet potatoes (17 per cent); cassava and maize were in an intermediate position (26 per cent and 33 per cent); it was highest in the case of beans (49 per cent), perhaps for the reason, among others, that beans are the most widely commercialised food product and the basis of the farmers' diet.

In principle, the use of selected seeds should increase the productivity of the land, but the effects are in fact almost insignificant. In Ruyigi, productivity was the same whether selected seeds[31] were used or not. In Ngozi the percentages were the same for low-productivity holdings (less than 20 000 FBu per hectare) but the percentage of holdings with production of over 40 000 FBu per hectare was slightly higher for users (24 per cent as against 20.4 per cent). Finally, in Bubanza, the high-productivity percentages were the same for user and non-user holdings, but the use of selected seeds reduced the proportion of low-productivity holdings (66.1 per cent instead of 75.7 per cent). The effect of selected seeds on land productivity is therefore noticeable, but not decisive. This is perhaps because seed selection is only one of a linked series of practices (fallowing, manuring, etc.) and so it is difficult to isolate its impact from that of these other variables. Only the combination of these practices can have an appreciable effect on the productivity of the land.

The study provides information on only one of these other techniques: anti-erosion works. The kinds of work required are different on the sloping land of the kind found in the hills of the interior and on the flat land of Bubanza. In the first case, it is necessary to protect the soil against rainfall erosion through reafforestation or through planting along the contour-lines. In the plain, wind-breaks are needed to prevent wind-erosion. The extent of this practice varied widely from region to region: 87.5 per cent of the Bubanza farmers never used them; 73.8 per cent in Ngozi and 34.5 per cent in Ruyigi had done so either in the year in question or in the preceding year. Two comments should be made: first, it is in the hill regions that the farmers see the most need for them; second, it is in Ngozi that the man-power needed to carry them out is the most readily available and the need for them is most evident. At the same time, while they can also have a favourable effect on yields, this is minor in comparison with the effects of the other techniques.

VI.   THE AGRICULTURAL WAGE-EARNERS

In an agricultural sector concerned mainly with subsistence, the wage-earner normally plays only a minor role, as each holding is worked by the labour of the family. Things change as cash crops are gradually introduced, as certain farmers expand their holdings and as agriculture becomes integrated into the market economy. This means that the role and nature of the wage-earner and such questions as the methods of payment are factors of considerable interest for learning about the evolution away from traditional agriculture.

In Burundi, wage-labour is still far from common. More than two-thirds of the farmers never employed labour from outside the family. The percentage varied widely from region to region, however, and even more from commune to commune. The gap between Bubanza and the interior of the country was particularly sharp, as shown in Table 27.

Table 27. **Employment of wage-labour per hectare, by region and commune**

Regions and communes	Percentages of respondents using wage-labour in the following ranges (days per hectare)					Total	
	0	1-19	20-49	50-99	≥100	%	Number of respondents
Bubanza	48.6	14.5	11.0	10.3	15.6	100	591
Rugombo	46.3	19.8	12.4	5.8	15.7	100	121
Buganda	41.1	15.5	13.2	13.2	17.0	100	129
Mpanda	53.3	13.2	10.6	10.6	12.3	100	227
Mutimbuzi	50.0	9.8	8.0	11.6	20.6	100	112
Other							2
Ngozi	79.7	10.7	4.3	3.7	1.6	100	512
Mwumba	78.5	12.6	5.1	2.5	1.3	100	79
Marangara	81.5	7.6	4.4	6.5	0.0	100	92
Kiremba	88.2	7.3	2.7	0.9	0.9	100	110
Ruhororo	71.8	12.8	6.0	6.8	2.6	100	117
Rango	78.9	13.2	3.5	1.8	2.6	100	114
Ruyigi	81.0	9.1	5.2	1.8	2.9	100	484
Ruyigi	75.8	12.6	7.4	3.2	1.0	100	95
Bweru	76.4	10.9	5.4	0.9	6.4	100	110
Musongati	87.1	4.9	5.0	2.0	1.0	100	101
Rutana	91.9	4.1	1.0	2.0	1.0	100	99
Kinyinya	72.1	13.9	7.6	1.3	5.1	100	79
Total	68.5	11.6	7.1	5.6	7.2	100	1 587

Whereas in the interior of the country 80 per cent of the farmers never employed wage-earners, the proportion was less than 50 per cent in Bubanza. The differences were even more marked at the commune level, with proportions of 91.9 per cent in Rutana and 41.1 per cent in Buganda. Closer examination of the degree of use for those holdings which do use wage-earners shows a progressively greater difference between regions as the degree of employment increases. Those holdings employing outsiders for less than 20 days per hectare were only slightly more numerous in Bubanza than in the interior, but holdings doing so for more than 50 days per hectare were fairly common in Bubanza (25.9 per cent) and rare in Ngozi and Ruyigi (5 per cent).

Even in Bubanza, however, this employment was hardly ever permanent – on only 3.9 per cent of holdings in Bubanza, 0.4 per cent in Ngozi and 1 per cent in Ruyigi. In fact there is virtually no such thing as a wage-earning class in the rural areas of Burundi. Most agricultural labourers, whether temporary or even permanent, are themselves owners of small plots, cultivated by their wives and children and providing the food necessary for the family. The temporary workers are active mainly at the peak periods of the farming year, either for the preparation of the fields (tilling), upkeep (weeding, mulching) or for harvest. In contrast, very few of them work in the dry season, from June to September, when Nature is dormant.

In a country as densely populated as Burundi, and especially in the most populous districts, the recruitment of this back-up labour force for the busy periods should not be difficult, particularly as the holdings are often tiny in relation to the work potential within the family itself. It should be particularly easy to find labour in the most densely populated areas. In fact, there maybe certain difficulties. In answer to the question "Is it very easy, easy, difficult or very difficult to find labour during the peak seasons?", 31.2 per cent of the farmers answered "difficult" or "very difficult" even in Ngozi. In Bubanza and Ruyigi, the difficulties were felt even more keenly, the corresponding proportions being 64.7 per cent and 51.5 per cent. These two regions are similarly placed concerning population density, but the problem is less easily soluble in Bubanza because the area of the holdings is often larger than the work capacity of the families installed on them, as a result of the special structure of the peasant communities.

Statistics on the wages earned by workers from outside the family confirm the gap between Bubanza and the interior of the country, as seen from Table 28.

Table 28. **Wage payments per holding, by region**

Region	Percentages of respondents making wage payments to outside labour in the following ranges: (FBU per year)				
	0	1 à 1 999	2 000 à 4 999	⩾5 000	Total
Bubanza	46.5	16.8	13	23.7	100
Ngozi	79.8	15.8	2.2	2.2	100
Ruyigi	81.8	12.6	2.7	2.9	100

The percentages of farmers spending little or nothing on wages were very similar in each of the three regions. At the other end of the scale, 36.7 per cent of the farmers in Bubanza spent more than 2 000 FBu, as against 4.4 per cent in Ngozi and 5.6 per cent in Ruyigi. This means that in the one case a fairly large number of farmers systematically employed wage labour, while in the other two regions the practice remained marginal. The difference results from the special nature of agriculture in Bubanza, which is the only region where a relative shortage of manpower (in relation to the size of holdings) is accompanied (thanks to the cash crops) by the existence of the monetary income needed to pay for it. This income is lacking in Ruyigi, while in Ngozi there is abundant labour within the family, due to over-population.

The methods of wage-payment vary among the regions. In Ruyigi 11.4 per cent and in Ngozi 6.5 per cent of farmers paid their labourers entirely or mainly in kind, but the practice was rare in Bubanza (3.3 per cent). In fact, the number of cases of payment in kind was greater there, since there are three times as many wage-labourers in the peasant communities of Bubanza as in Ngozi or Ruyigi. It is only here that sufficient money is available to permit the development of a new class of agricultural wage-earners, thanks to the cash crops and the resulting modernisation of the economy. But it should not be forgotten that these labourers have a dual status, with their resources coming both from tiny holdings and temporary employment. Even in Bubanza the permanent wage-earners (virtually non-existent elsewhere) represented only an insignificant proportion of the active population (less than 5 per cent).

The advantage enjoyed by Bubanza over the regions of the interior concerning the availability of money leads also to the differences in average wages shown in Table 29.

The highest wages were paid in Bubanza, where 62.6 per cent of the labourers earned more than 40 FBu a day, compared with 20.2 per cent in Ngozi and 24.7 per cent in Ruyigi. It is true that a small number of labourers (8 to 10 per cent) were paid at the same low rates in all

Table 29. **Average daily wage, by region**

Region	Average per day of work (FBU)	Percentages of respondents paying daily wages to outside workers in the following ranges: (FBU)				Total	
		1-19	20-39	40-59	≥60	%	Number of respondents
Bubanza	51	8.4	29.0	40.7	21.9	100	297
Ngozi	47	10.1	69.7	7.1	13.1	100	99
Ruyigi	36[1]	10.6	64.7	5.9	18.8	100	85
Total		9.1	43.7	27.7	19.5	100	481

1. This figure has been corrected for three abnormal values (included in the distributional data).

three regions, but the modal wage was in the 40-60 FBu range in Bubanza and in the 20-40 FBu range in the other two regions. This difference is closely parallelled by what the farmers in different regions see as "a fair wage": in Bubanza 66.3 per cent indicated a figure in the range 40-60 FBu, while 80.9 per cent in Ngozi and 89.3 per cent in Ruyigi indicated between 20 and 40 FBu.

Finally, an important relationship between use of wage-labour and land productivity must be underlined. In each region, the number of days of wage-labour per hectare increased with increases in this productivity, as shown in Table 30.

In each region, the percentage of holdings with production per hectare less than 20 000 FBu fell as use of wage-labour rose. For zero days and 60 or more per year, the

Table 30. **Productivity per hectare of cultivated land and use of wage-labour**

Days of outside labour per hectare of cultivated land, by region	Percentages of respondents with values of production per hectare in the following ranges: (FBU)			Total	
	0-19 999	20 000-39 999	≥40 000	%	Number of respondents
Bubanza	70.0	23.4	6.6	100	591
0	75.6	16.7	7.7	100	287
1-29	84.5	13.6	1.8	100	110
30-59	60.4	35.8	3.8	100	53
≥60	51.1	39.7	9.2	100	141
Ngozi	47.5	30.3	22.3	100	512
0	48.5	30.4	21.1	100	408
1-29	48.5	33.8	17.7	100	68
30-59	43.7	25.0	31.3	100	16
≥60	25.0	20.0	55.0	100	20
Ruyigi	62.4	24.6	13.0	100	484
0	49.2	20.4	11.4	100	392
1-29	87.3	10.9	1.8	100	55
30-59	56.2	25.0	18.8	100	16
≥60	33.3	47.6	19.1	100	21
Total	60.4	26.0	13.6	100	1 587

proportions went from 75.6 per cent to 51.1 per cent in Bubanza, from 48.5 per cent to 25 per cent in Ngozi and from 49.2 per cent to 33.3 per cent in Ruyigi. The association was equally clear in the case of high-productivity holdings (production per hectare over 40 000 FBu) in Ngozi and Ruyigi, where the proportions increased with the input of wage-labour: 55 per cent and 19.1 per cent for 60 days or more as against 21.1 per cent and 11.4 per cent for zero days. This relationship has a dual significance: the role of wage-labour increases as production becomes better organised, as management improves, as the choice of crops approaches the optimum combination; at the same time, as productivity increases the farmer has available more of the resources needed to pay for the labour. The development of wage-labour is therefore both one of the factors in the growth of productivity and one of its consequences.

Many details concerning the behaviour of the farmers confirmed that the use of wage-labour is only one of many elements involved in the evolution in mentalities and the transformation of agricultural practices. The farmer who took on labour and made a profit out of it was more aware and better-informed than the others. Those who listened frequently to the radio derived an average profit of 8.9 FBu per day and per outside worker, whereas those who listened rarely or never showed losses of 17.4 FBu or 35.9 FBu, depending on the method of calculation used. The method of payment (in cash or in kind) combined with the degree of integration into the market economy was shown to be a good guide to the profit of the farmer. Those who listened frequently to the radio realised a high profit if they were also among those who paid in cash, but a low one if they paid in kind. Those who never listened made small losses if they paid in cash (2.3 FBu to 5.7 FBu) but large ones (50.5 FBu to 251.2 FBu) if in kind.

Education levels also have a significant effect on the profits obtained from employing labour. Those with low levels (people who never went to school, but who can sometimes read and write) managed their holdings less rationally than the others. In fact, their profit amounted to only 4.2 FBu a day, compared with 14.6 FBu for those who had gone beyond primary level. These results agree with those presented earlier in showing that the decision to use wage-labour is more rational from an economic point of view when the farmer is better-informed and better-educated.

VII. SUPPORTING SERVICES, ENVIRONMENT AND EFFICIENCY

The study unearthed a wide range of information on social variables such as religious practices, relations with the political authorities, access to information, etc. As a result it was possible to study in depth not only the impact of supporting services on the nature and efficiency of farm management, but also that of numerous social, cultural and political variables.

A. Supporting services

The farmers are able to have direct contacts with the extension workers or the agronomists, but not with the agronomic experts trained in the Faculté d'Agronomie, whose time is completely taken up with administrative and political tasks. The extension worker is normally the son of a farmer who has received an accelerated training and whose job is to supervise the growing of cotton and coffee and to give advice to the farmers on how to obtain the best yields. These extension workers are themselves supervised by the agronomists, who have received a more thorough training at the Institut des Techniques Agricoles du Burundi (ITAB), the only institution training middle-level managers for agriculture.

Bubanza is the region where the farmers reported having the most contact with the extension workers. For 77.2 per cent of them these contacts were frequent. The proportion was even higher (over 81 per cent) in the two communes with rice- and cotton-growing peasant communities run with outside technical assistance. In Ngozi, intensive support was less important (63.5 per cent), while in Ruyigi, the region with least cash crops, the proportion was only 37.4 per cent. Support from the agronomists showed a similar pattern, although the differences between the regions were even more marked, the proportion of farmers with frequent contacts ranging from 50.1 per cent in Bubanza to 26.1 per cent in Ngozi and 10.3 per cent in Ruyigi. Outside support is therefore more common in areas where there is a higher share of cash crops in total agricultural production. The percentage was 6 or 7 points higher for farmers with close supervision and support than for those with little or none. This association with cash crops comes out even more strongly if one takes the figures for expenditure per adult in each household (which are highly dependent on the monetary income of the holding). These came to 2 704 FBu for those with no contact with the extension workers (2 649 FBu in the case of the agronomists) and 4 852 FBu for those with frequent contacts (6 443 FBu for the agronomists). These figures show that the supporting services, especially the agronomists, can bring about greater integration into the market economy.

On the other hand, their impact on efficiency of management (as measured by productivity per hectare) was apparent only in Bubanza, as shown in Table 31.

The farmers in Bubanza who maintained close contacts with the extension workers achieved better results than those having none at all. The proportions of holdings with productivity per hectare below 20 000 FBu and over 40 000 FBu were 68.9 per cent and 7 per cent respectively in the first case and 75 per cent and 4.2 per cent in the second. In Ngozi and Ruyigi, however, the percentages with or without outside support were almost identical.

Table 31. **Degree of external support and productivity per hectare of cultivated land**

Frequency of respondent's contacts with extension workers, by region	Percentages of respondents with values of production per hectare in the following ranges: (FBU)			Total	
	0-19 999	20 000-39 999	⩾40 000	%	Number of respondents
Bubanza					
Frequent contact	68.9	24.1	7.0	100	456
Infrequent contact	71.8	20.5	7.7	100	39
No contact	75.0	20.8	4.2	100	96
Ngozi					
Frequent contact	47.7	31.1	21.2	100	325
Infrequent contact	42.9	25.0	32.1	100	28
No contact	47.8	29.6	22.6	100	159
Ruyigi					
Frequent contact	61.9	24.3	13.8	100	181
Infrequent contact	67.2	16.4	16.4	100	61
No contact	61.6	26.9	11.5	100	242

B. Education and the desire for education

As in all developing countries, the role played by children in the family holding is appreciable. This means that the more time they spend in school, the smaller the contribution they can make to production. It even raises the question whether, as a result, productivity per hectare should not be expected to decline as the rate of school attendance increases. Such a hypothesis was confirmed by the study as far as the regions of the interior are concerned, but contradicted in the case of Bubanza. The proportions of total holdings with production per hectare of over 40 000 FBu fell from 23.1 per cent (Ngozi) and 13.1 per cent (Ruyigi) in cases where no child was attending school to 14.6 per cent and 11.6 per cent in cases where one or more children attended. Conversely, the proportions of low-productivity holdings (less than 20 000 FBu) rose from 47.3 per cent to 50 per cent in Ngozi and from 60.3 per cent to 65.1 per cent in Ruyigi when the number of children at school went from 0 to 1 or more. In contrast, the variations in Bubanza were of the same order, but in the opposite direction.

The relationship between productivity and the desire for education is quite different and turned out to be rather complex. The farmers who ran their holdings best (achieving above-average productivity per hectare) were the ones who most easily saw their sons following the same calling as themselves but they were also the ones who wanted the longest schooling for their children.

In general, the farmers who wanted their children to have a career outside agriculture were slightly more numerous than those who did not. It is logical that those who would choose the same activity for their children should be most often found among the farmers whose holdings were the most profitable. Thus, for the high-productivity holdings (over 40 000 FBu per hectare) the percentage of farmers who would like their sons to follow the same calling was 8.7 per cent in Bubanza and 24.2 per cent in Ruyigi, compared with 5.3 per cent and 20.4 per cent who wished the opposite. On the other hand, the families desiring to change their condition predominated among those with low-productivity holdings. In Ruyigi, however, the farmers' attitudes were somewhat different, the desire for change being as frequently expressed by those with above-average productivity. It is true that agricultural income per active worker in this region, where cash crops are marginal, is far lower than that recorded in the other two regions. This shortfall may explain the desire for change even on the part of the most efficient farmers.

The best way to find a different kind of career is obviously through the school. The study showed the extent of the farmers' ambitions on this point: 80.8 per cent of the respondents said they would like their children to continue at school at least up to secondary level. Of these, 58.3 per cent went further and wanted to see their sons go on to higher education. In each region the farmers with modest ambitions for their children (primary or technical) were in the majority in the group with low productivity per hectare while the more ambitious ones (secondary or higher) predominated in the high-productivity group. This is easily explained. The farmers who are most efficient and can therefore make a surplus are the ones who can afford to pay for their children's studies, even if they last a long time. This will probably have an unfavourable effect on agriculture, since it means that the know-how of the most competent farmers is not being passed on to the next generation, even if these are the ones who say they least envisage that their children should give up farming.

C. Social integration

The modernisation of agriculture depends partly on the attitudes of farmers to technical progress, their access to information, and their relations with the political and administrative authorities, because of their key role in the distribution of fertilizer, selected seeds or advanced tools. It is therefore of interest to discover the influence of these different variables on the way holdings are managed and on the income of the farmers.

Relations with the authorities were measured by the frequency of contacts with the district commissioner and the provincial government. In the first case, there was a positive relationship, admittedly only moderate, with productivity per hectare in Bubanza and Ngozi, but a negative one in Ruyigi. In all three regions, however, there was a positive and much more definite relationship, if relations with the provincial governor are taken separately. The more frequent the contact, the higher the productivity per hectare of the farmers concerned.Of the farmers having no contact, 72.2 per cent (Bubanza), 59.1 per cent (Ngozi) and 60.8 per cent (Ruyigi) were in the low-productivity category, while the corresponding figures for farmers with frequent contacts were much lower (59.4 per cent, 62.5 per cent and 56.8 per cent respectively)[32].

Listening to the radio and reading newspapers are the two essential forms of access to information. On the hypothesis that technical progress and innovation are more readily accepted in well-informed families than in those which live turned in on themselves, without contacts with the authorities and away from the mass media, there should be a relationship between access to the media and the management of holdings. In practice, relatively few people read newspapers (only 21.9 per cent of respondents read them at one time or another); the radio was therefore the dominant channel of information (83.6 per cent of respondents listened to it).

Table 32 would seem to confirm the thesis that information has a favourable effect on productivity.

In each region, production per hectare increased with the frequency of listening to the radio. The variations were in fact quite important, since among farmers who never listened the low and high productivity proportions were: 85.9 per cent and 1.6 per cent (Bubanza); 55.2 per cent and 10.3 per cent (Ngozi); 65.7 per cent and 10.4 per cent (Ruyigi). The

Table 32. **Frequency of listening to the radio and productivity per hectare of cultivated land**

Frequency of listening to the radio, by region	Percentages of respondents with values of production per hectare in the following ranges: (FBU)			Total	
	0-19 999	20 000-39 999	≥40 000	%	Number of respondents
Bubanza	70.0	23.3	6.4	100	591
Often	67.4	23.3	9.3	100	270
Not so often	68.9	26.1	5.0	100	257
Never	85.9	12.5	1.6	100	64
Ngozi	47.3	30.4	22.2	100	509
Often	42.1	35.8	22.1	100	159
Not so often	48.6	26.7	24.7	100	292
Never	55.2	34.5	10.3	100	58
Ruyigi	62.7	24.2	13.0	100	482
Often	60.9	22.8	16.3	100	92
Not so often	61.7	25.0	13.3	100	256
Never	65.7	23.9	10.4	100	134

corresponding figures for frequent listeners were: 67.4 per cent and 9.3 per cent (Ngozi); 42.1 per cent and 22.1 per cent (Ngozi); 60.9 per cent and 16.3 per cent (Ruyigi).

The link between information and productivity came out much less strongly in the case of newspaper-reading, which admittedly concerned only a minority of farmers. In Ngozi and Ruyigi, farmers achieving high productivity were proportionately more numerous among newspaper-readers than among non-readers, but the reverse was true in Bubanza where much closer outside support may perhaps provide a substitute, as far as information is concerned, for newspaper-reading.

While access to information and contact with the authorities clearly exert an influence, the behaviour of the farmers also depends on their own attitudes to change and their own aspirations to progress, which may themselves be linked to the desire to be better informed. In fact, to the question "What does progress mean to you?", half the respondents replied "the improvement of production and/or the standard of living". In two of the regions, Bubanza and Ngozi, this reply came relatively more frequently from high-productivity farmers, but in Ruyigi the tendency was reversed, perhaps because the virtual absence of cash crops in this region is not compatible with the idea of economic progress associated with improvement in the standard of living.

D. Traditional and modern beliefs

Are rational behaviour and efficient management of holdings linked to a modern mentality? If so, traditional beliefs might be expected to form an obstacle to modernisation and progress in agriculture. This hypothesis requires to be tested extremely carefully in order to avoid reaching heavily-loaded but not fully substantiated conclusions.

The first cultural variable to be examined was religious persuasion, shown in Table 33.

In two of the regions, Bubanza and Ngozi, the religious factor seemed to be significant. Production per hectare was higher on holdings run by followers of one of the Western religions (Catholic or Protestant) than on those owned by animists. The phenomenon was particularly evident in Bubanza.

On the other hand, in Ruyigi, the most traditionalist of the three regions, followers of the Western religions appeared to be more numerous in the low-productivity category than the animists, the leading group in the high-productivity category.

What may be a more decisive influence in modifying traditional behaviour is the degree of religious observance. Farmers who regularly attend Mass or other services are plainly more exposed to the cultural influences accompanying the practice of Western religions than are the farmers who go to church only a few times a year at the time of the major festivals or for important family events. The study showed that farmers attending church regularly did indeed achieve higher productivities on their holdings. The strength of this conclusion was the same for each region. For the three regions together, 57.4 per cent of regular churchgoers were in the low-productivity category (less than 20 000 FBu per hectare) and 15.4 per cent had high productivity (more than 40 000 FBu per hectare), whereas for those who went rarely or never the proportions were 66.7 per cent and 8.2 per cent respectively. These results are in agreement with the data in Table 33. Indeed, if Western religions lead to more rational behaviour (taken strictly in the Western sense of the term) in production matters, it is only to be expected that this influence should increase with the regularity with which the faithful practise their religion.

62

Table 33. **Religion and production per hectare of cultivated land**

Religion of the respondent, by region	Percentages of respondents with values of production per hectare in the following ranges: (FBU)			Total	
	0-19 999	20 000-39 999	≥40 000	%	Number of respondents
Bubanza	70.0	23.4	6.6	100	586
Christian					
(Catholic or Protestant)	67.3	25.3	7.4	100	474
Traditional	81.0	16.0	3.0	100	100
Ngozi	47.5	30.3	22.2	100	508
Christian					
(Catholic or Protestant)	47.3	30.3	22.4	100	478
Traditional	47.8	34.8	17.4	100	23
Ruyigi	62.3	24.6	13.1	100	483
Christian					
(Catholic or Protestant)	63.2	24.4	12.4	100	372
Traditional	59.9	25.2	15.0	100	107
All three regions	60.4	26.0	13.6	100	1 577
Christian					
(Catholic or Protestant)	58.9	26.9	14.2	100	1 324
Traditional	67.8	22.2	10.0	100	230

Other variables made it possible to assess the influence of traditional beliefs on the farmers' behaviour. This is particularly the case for food tabus. In the traditional society, women would not eat eggs for fear this would affect their fertility. This refusal has persisted to the present day and remains strongest where mentalities have been least influenced by modern elements: 73.8 per cent of the women in Ruyigi followed this practice, but only 57.6 per cent in Ngozi and no more than 46.4 per cent in Bubanza. In all three regions, women who refused to eat eggs were proportionately more numerous in the low-productivity categories and, with the exception of Bubanza, least numerous on high-productivity holdings.

The second food tabu concerns sheep-meat and affects men and women equally. According to the traditional beliefs, the sheep is a sacred animal and it would therefore be sacrilege to kill it and eat its flesh. This ban was less widely observed than the egg tabu, but was nevertheless respected by the majority of farmers (58.4 per cent) in Ruyigi, as against 23 per cent in Ngozi and 48.4 per cent in Bubanza, where the relatively high figure is perhaps explained by the relative unimportance of livestock.

It was only in Bubanza and Ngozi that respect for this tradition turned out to be associated with lower productivity. In these two regions, farmers failing to respect the ban were relatively more likely to achieve high productivity (more than 40 000 FBu per hectare) than the traditionalists. The percentage differences are slight, however.

The only cultural factor capable of influencing farmers' behaviour therefore seems to be the choice between new faiths, Western in origin, and traditional beliefs (and practices).

VIII. NON-AGRICULTURAL INCOME AND ACTIVITIES

Before examining the total incomes and expenditures of the households, it may be useful to discuss the outside activities of certain members of the farming community and the incomes which they bring in, since these form part of the total income.

In a traditional subsistence economy, outside activities normally play only a marginal role: farmers do not have enough money to pay even temporary labour; the urban sector is insignificant and provides only a tiny number of jobs for the rural population living near the towns. But in Burundi the economy and, in certain regions, agriculture are already sufficiently developed for the towns and even the agricultural sector to be able to offer a certain number of jobs to farming families. The analysis of these jobs and the resulting incomes is therefore of interest in measuring this development which, it turns out, differs widely between regions.

As Table 34 shows, wage-earning attained very different proportions in different communes, ranging from 6 per cent of the respondents' families in Rutana to 37.9 per cent in Mpanda, the commune closest to the capital. It depends partly, therefore, on proximity to the town. It was highest (22.8 per cent) in Bubanza because of the strong pull exerted by the capital, Bujumbura, and the job possibilities it offers. The strength of this pull is in fact a function of distance. The wage-earning proportions were lowest (10 to 11 per cent, of the same

Table 34. **Adult members of households working away from the farm,
by region and commune** [1]

| Region and commune | Percentages of respondents with the following numbers of adults working off the farm: | | | Total | |
	0	1	≥2	%	Number of respondents
Bubanza	77.2	16.6	6.2	100	591
Rugombo	90.1	9.1	0.8	100	121
Buganda	89.1	10.1	0.8	100	129
Mpanda	62.1	23.8	14.1	100	227
Mutimbuzi	79.5	17.9	2.6	100	112
Other					
Ngozi	87.1	11.1	1.8	100	512
Mwumba	92.4	6.3	1.3	100	79
Marangara	83.7	16.3	0.0	100	92
Kiremba	90.0	10.0	0.0	100	110
Ruhororo	82.9	13.7	3.4	100	117
Rango	87.7	8.8	3.5	100	114
Ruyigi	90.7	7.2	2.1	100	484
Ruyigi	87.4	8.4	4.2	100	95
Bweru	90.9	7.3	1.8	100	110
Musongati	93.1	5.0	1.9	100	101
Rutana	94.0	4.0	2.0	100	99
Kinyinya	87.3	12.7	0.0	100	79
Total	84.5	12.0	3.5	100	1 587

1. Children under 15 are counted as half an adult.

order as in the regions of the interior) in the two communes which are furthest away from Bujumbura (Buganda and Rugombo).

The proportion in Ngozi, 12.9 per cent, was higher than in Ruyigi, 9.3 per cent, because of over-population in the hill-districts of the region. The farmers are therefore forced by the shortage of land to seek other sources of income. In all, with the exception of some of the Ruyigi communes, outside activities were shown to be no longer negligible, since 10 to 15 per cent of families were involved. They were of great importance in the two communes closest to Bujumbura, affecting 20.5 per cent and 37.9 per cent of families. These two communes represent a fairly advanced stage of the transformation of rural society, with Rutana, at the other end of the scale, still typifying the traditional rural society.

In order to grasp the real importance of the modern wage-earners, a more precise and so more satisfactory indicator is the ratio between the number of days worked off the farm to the number of days worked both on and off. The variations between regions and communes for this indicator were practically the same as for the earlier one. Rutana, with a figure of zero for 94.9 per cent of families, and Mpanda (zero in the case of 64.8 per cent) were still at the two extremes. Bubanza again stood apart, with 79.5 per cent of families reporting a figure of zero, compared with 89.5 per cent in Ngozi and 92 per cent in Ruyigi. The ratio lay between 1 per cent and 29 per cent for most of the other families, rarely exceeding 30 per cent except in the two communes neighbouring on Bujumbura (8.8 per cent and 8.9 per cent of families). The gap between these communes and those situated in the interior therefore came out even more strongly using this indicator, which gives a more precise measure of the relative importance of outside activities. The strong inclination of the inhabitants of the two communes of Mpanda and Mutimbuzi to work outside is the result of a combination of several factors: first, the convenience of access to the town, easily reached by bicycle or even on foot. The system of motor roads laid out at the same time as the peasant communities is highly developed throughout Bubanza, which makes it easy to move about. In addition, local agriculture is mainly market-oriented: as well as selling their cotton and coffee, the Bubanza farmers supply the Bujumbura market with various food products such as maize, cassava, sweet potatoes, bananas, beans, and sorghum. The situation in the regions of the interior is quite different: there are few contacts with Bujumbura, because it is so far away; townships in the interior are insignificant and offer few job possibilities; finally, the local farmers, especially in Ruyigi, are much more involved in a traditional form of agriculture, based on subsistence.

It should be underlined, however, that in each of the regions, including Bubanza, the town provides only a minority of the jobs concerned. In most cases the member of the family who works elsewhere is an agricultural labourer, as shown in Table 35.

It is worth pointing out, first of all, as shown by the figures in the last line of the table, that in absolute terms Bubanza provided more than three times as many outside jobs as the regions of the interior. The same distribution of jobs therefore implies three times as many urban jobs as elsewhere.

In Bubanza, the large number of outside workers in agriculture is the result of the agrarian structure. The average size of holding is much larger there than in the other two regions and the man-power available within the family therefore often turns out to be insufficient. In addition, the organisation of the peasant communities implies the creation of many posts (extension workers, weights and measures officials, overseers, accountants, etc.) which explains the high figure for public officials. On the other hand, since trading is carried out by para-statal organisations, this activity provides few opportunities (only 2.1 per cent were traders or craftsmen) in spite of the fact that many farmers, as they made clear during the interviews, would like to exercise this type of activity to improve their standard of living. At the other extreme, shortage of land in relation to the man-power available within the family

Table 35. **Activity of members of the household working outside, by region**

Type of activity	Percentages in the activities shown:			
	Bubanza	Ngozi	Ruyigi	Total
1. Agricultural workers	72.7	58.8	75.0	69.6
2. Administrative officials	10.2	13.7	3.6	9.9
3. Domestic workers	9.1	10.0	10.7	9.6
4. Traders and craftsmen	2.1	12.5	7.1	5.6
5. Other	5.9	5.0	3.6	5.3
Total : .... %	100	100	100	100
.... Number of observations	187	80	56	323

explains the low percentage of agricultural wage-earners in Ngozi (58.8 per cent as against three-quarters in the other two regions). It is in this region that the proportions of jobs in administration (13.7 per cent) and commerce and crafts (12.5 per cent) were highest, the consequence of the predominant situation of coffee in the local economy. This crop, by its nature, involves numerous commercial activities. In addition, the monetisation of the economy in the region favours the expansion of the administrative system, especially for controlling the production and marketing of coffee. Activities of this kind create relatively fewer jobs in Ruyigi, where coffee plays only a minor role. The share of agricultural wage-earners is consequently large (75 per cent), partly also as the result of the absence of surplus family labour in relation to the available areas.

These results are confirmed by the part of the study dealing with the non-agricultural activities of family members (in other words, outside activities other than as agricultural workers). The share of trade was highest in Ngozi (32.9 per cent) and lowest in Ruyigi (19.6 per cent). The fact that crafts predominated in Ruyigi (32.1 per cent as against 21 per cent elsewhere) is partly due to the more restricted distribution of manufactured goods in this under-monetised region. Finally, it was in Bubanza that the share of jobs in the service sector, excluding commerce, was highest, because of the possibilities offered by the capital.

In all three regions examined, as in many African countries, education plays a vital role in the employment of man-power from rural areas in non-agricultural activities. Table 36 shows clearly that the tendency to work outside the holding increases with the level of education.

In each region, the people working on the holding had for the most part never been to school[33]. On the other hand, the proportion of those working outside who had never had any education was 42.4 per cent in Bubanza and 26.3 per cent in Ruyigi. Going further, those working on the holding were less often people who had had prolonged (3-6 years) primary or secondary education than in the case of those who worked outside: in Bubanza, 31.6 per cent compared with 51.9 per cent; in Ngozi 37.6 per cent and 55.3 per cent. Only in Ruyigi were the percentages the same. Here, the situation results from the limited possibilities of outside employment and the abundance of cultivable land, which means that there is no pressure to seek jobs outside the holdings, as is the case in Ngozi. But in the other two regions, including Bubanza, which is the only one where outside employment has really been developed, education clearly prepares the children of farming families for finding jobs outside the holding, particularly non-agricultural jobs for which a minimum of education is an essential entry requirement.

66

Table 36. **Education levels of people working on or outside the holding**

| Region | Percentages of respondents or members of households with the following levels of education | | | | Total | |
	No school attendance	Yaga 1-3/ Primary 1-2	Yaga 4-6/ Primary 3-6	Secondary or beyond	%	Number of respondents
Bubanza						
Working on the holding	61.9	6.5	28.7	2.9	100	485
Working outside	42.4	5.7	39.6	12.3	100	106
Ngozi						
Working on the holding	50.2	12.2	36.5	1.1	100	474
Working outside	26.3	18.4	52.6	2.7	100	38
Ruyigi						
Working on the holding	65.9	12.4	19.5	2.2	100	451
Working outside	63.6	15.2	21.2	–	100	33
All three regions						
Working on the holding	59.2	10.3	28.4	2.1	100	1 410
Working outside	42.9	10.2	39.0	7.9	100	177

The income brought into the household by the outside activities is very small compared with other sources. Whereas the annual average income per household was over 27 000 FBu in Bubanza and Ngozi and 19 700 FBu in Ruyigi, two-thirds of the families with outside activities made less than 5 000 FBu out of them. This category of low earnings from outside activities was largest in Ruyigi (81 per cent, compared with 63.5 per cent in Ngozi and 59.3 per cent in Bubanza). In two cases out of three, therefore, outside labour accounted for less than one-fifth of the total household income. The smallness of this contribution to family income stems from the temporary nature of most of the work. The monthly income of outside workers was 2 140 FBu in Bubanza, 970 FBu in Ngozi and 600 FBu in Ruyigi, but the jobs concerned were available for only two or three months in the year. The higher figure for Bubanza results from the possibility, at least for a minority, of finding jobs in Bujumbura where the wage-levels are much higher than in the rest of the country. In addition, even the rural wage-levels in this part of the country are sustained by a relative shortage of man-power. In Ngozi, on the other hand, the permanent surplus of man-power keeps agricultural wage-levels down. The situation is quite different in Ruyigi where the low wage-levels are the result, not of over-supply, but of a shortage of demand in an essentially non-monetised economy where family labour makes up most of the work-force.

It is also interesting to note that the "fair wage" as estimated by the farmers depends on the actual wage-level. More than 4 farmers out of 5 in Bubanza considered that the fair wage was between 1 000 and 2 000 FBu per month; in the other two regions the subjective "fair wage" was appreciably lower, with 3 farmers out of 5 putting it between 500 and 1 000 FBu per month.

The last point requiring detailed analysis concerns the impact of outside work on the way the holdings are managed. A priori, one might hope to see two favourable effects, one on the level of investment, the other on the evolution of techniques. It is clear that an outside activity brings in additional resources and so favours the families concerned over those with similar sizes of holding but no outside income. As a result, outside activities ought to enable these families to finance investment more easily than the others. At the same time, outside activities can bring in new knowledge, new practices, know-how from "learning by doing" and break the isolation of farming families who previously could only follow, if not tradition, at least the ancestral techniques. Temporary employment on a larger holding where cash crops are being developed, or a job in the town with the resulting access to information, should favour the introduction of new techniques, improved management and the opening up of the holding to market forces.

In practice, outside work, barring certain exceptions, is favourable to productivity increases, as shown in Table 37.

Table 37. **Extent of outside work and productivity per hectare, by region**

Outside work as percentage of work on the holding	Percentages of holdings with values of production per hectare in the following ranges: (FBU)			Total	
	0-19 999	20 000-39 999	⩾40 000	%	Number of respondents
Bubanza	70.0	23.4	6.6	100	591
0	71.7	22.8	5.5	100	470
1-9	60.5	25.6	13.9	100	43
⩾10	65.4	25.6	9.0	100	78
Ngozi	47.5	30.3	22.2	100	512
0	47.6	30.8	21.6	100	458
1-9	63.0	19.8	22.2	100	27
⩾10	29.6	37.0	33.4	100	27
Ruyigi	62.4	24.6	13.0	100	484
0	61.6	25.2	13.2	100	445
1-9	76.9	15.4	7.7	100	26
⩾10	61.5	23.1	15.4	100	13
Total	60.4	26.0	13.6	100	1 587

In Bubanza and Ngozi, there seemed to be confirmation of the favourable effects of outside work. In Bubanza, the highest proportion of the low-productivity group (71.7 per cent) and the lowest proportion of the high-productivity group (5.5 per cent) were accounted for by families with no member working outside. In Ngozi, there was a substantial difference between the productivity of those holdings where there was no outside activity and those where it exceeded 10 per cent of the total work done. In Ruyigi, however, the variations in productivity bore no significant relation to the amount of outside work. This lack of association may perhaps be caused by the kind of jobs available in the region and the incapacity of subsistence agriculture to make innovations through contacts with the outside world. The results from Bubanza and Ngozi are nevertheless enough to confirm that outside activities not only bring in additional income but also induce more progressive behaviour on the part of the farmers.

IX. TOTAL INCOME AND EXPENDITURE

After examining the non-agricultural income received by a minority of farming families and the nature and cost of the inputs used for agricultural production, it is now possible to proceed to a synthesis of this information in the present chapter dealing with the total income and expenditure of the families.

A. *Total income*

Section III (Table 11) gave details of the value of agricultural production in each region, as well as its dispersion. This is the gross income from which must be deducted all production expenses (wages of non-family workers, rent for land, payments for fertilizer, selected seeds, use of machines, irrigation, extension and finally depreciation of tools) to arrive at net income. This income does not necessarily correspond to the total net income of the families, since some families receive income other than through the holding. Three concepts must be distinguished:

1. gross agricultural income
2. net agricultural income = (1) – expenditure on inputs
3. total net income = (2) + income from outside (wages and rents).

Table 38 presents the data for each of these concepts for each region together with their dispersion.

Table 38. **Agricultural income, gross and net,
and total net income, by region**

Region	Average total income per household, net (FBU)	Average agricultural income per household, net (FBU)	Agricultural income per household, net (FBU)			Number of observations	
			Average	Median	Standard deviation	Respondents	% of total
Bubanza	26 103	23 465	29 682	23 091	26 613	588	37
Ngozi	28 656	27 947	29 092	25 212	21 644	508	32
Ruyigi	19 665	19 197	20 341	16 437	17 902	484	31
Total	24 955	23 600	26 628	21 505	23 006	1 580	100

The table shows a sharp split between Bubanza and the regions of the interior, i.e. between a region where gross agricultural income, net agricultural income and total net income were quite different and two regions where they were nearly identical. This split is evidence of two features specific to the Bubanza region: it is the only one where the cost of inputs was substantial (21 per cent of gross income) and the only one where income from outside the holding was other than negligible (11.3 per cent of net agricultural income, against 2.5 per cent in the interior).

Running costs amounted to 6 217 FBu in Bubanza compared with 1 145 FBu in the interior. The difference of about 5 000 FBu is mainly accounted for by the annual dues paid by the farmers to the regional development corporations for their services (extension, supply of fertilizer, seeds, use of machinery, etc.). The result is that the Bubanza farmers, although their holdings are on average twice as large as those of Ngozi, had appreciably lower net average incomes (23 465 FBu compared with 27 947 FBu, a difference of 16 per cent). Admittedly this income is substantially higher than that of a region with a traditional subsistence economy (22 per cent higher than the net agricultural income in Ruyigi), but it may still seem paradoxical that the average net income on holdings which are both much larger and have available a whole range of modern techniques through the regional development corporations should be lower than in Ngozi, a region suffering from land shortage and a virtual absence of technical support.

In fact, as was pointed out in Chapter 3, the value of cotton and rice production, the main cash crops in Bubanza, is substantially under-estimated because of the State-imposed price system, which is not true of coffee. Doubling the prices for cotton and rice would increase net income by nearly 8 800 FBu, bringing it up to 32 200 FBu and exceeding the net income in Ngozi by 15 per cent[34].

The comparison between the two regions of the interior suffers from no such distortion. In spite of population pressure, the absence of modern techniques and a low average size of holding, the impact of coffee-growing is such that net income in Ngozi, at 27 947 FBu was 45 per cent higher than in Ruyigi (19 197 FBu). This advantage stems from a major difference in gross revenues without any offsetting difference in production costs, equal in the two regions. This means that without any modernisation of techniques and in spite of an unfavourable average area per holding, coffee allows net agricultural income to be raised by half.

In the regions of the interior, total income was virtually equal to net agricultural income, given the small incomes from outside the holding (709 FBu and 468 FBu), but these figures are averages and there are in practice two types of holding: in one, accounting for about 90 per cent of cases, the supplementary income was zero; in the other 10 per cent, the additional sums were far from negligible (about 25 per cent of total income for both regions). The farmers benefiting from these additional incomes accounted for different proportions depending on whether the net income was low (less than 20 000 FBu), in which case it was 13 per cent, medium (20 000 to 40 000 FBu), or high (over 40 000 FBu), for which the figures were 10 per cent and 18 per cent respectively. Furthermore, in the first of these groups the additional income was small (less than 5 000 FBu) for eight families out of ten, whereas for the same proportion in the third group the addition was more than 5 000 FBu. This means that there are two distinct categories of outside income. In one case, some of the poorest farmers are obliged to offer their services for very low wages, because their small holdings cannot cover the basic needs of their families; in the other, country-dwellers who are already well-informed and who have probably had a minimum of education have managed to find relatively well-paid jobs in the town.

In Bubanza, the outside income amounted to 2 638 FBu or nearly four times the Ngozi figure. This appreciably narrows the income gap between the regions, since total incomes in Bubanza were on average 9 per cent below Ngozi's, while net agricultural incomes were 16 per cent lower. It is probable that on certain holdings the additional money is indispensable for the payment of running costs in bad years. The farmers in this region in fact have an obvious geographic advantage through their proximity to Bujumbura, providing incomes which are out of reach of the other two regions. This advantage, however, can in no way justify the pricing policy of the State, which means that the farmers fail to derive more than partial benefit from the commercialisation and modernisation of agriculture which, under normal conditions – in other words, free pricing – would provide them with the highest net income in Burundi outside the towns.

The distribution of incomes, already fairly uneven, with a Gini coefficient of 0.45 for the three regions together, does not depend on the presence or absence of cash crops. The highest and lowest concentrations were to be found in Bubanza (Gini 0.50) and Ngozi (Gini 0.36), with Ruyigi in between (Gini 0.45). In Bubanza half the farmers received only 16 per cent of the total gross income, while the most prosperous 20 per cent received 53 per cent. The ratio between the average incomes of the two groups was therefore 8.3 to 1. This shows that average values are more or less meaningless in this region and throws doubt on the policies of the regional development corporations. In principle, each family should have the same advantages in terms of size of holding and outside help, but in fact there are substantial differences in gross income between the farmers. In Ngozi the land shortage means that medium-sized holdings are rare and this explains the smaller disparities, the poorest half receiving 23 per cent and the richest group, 41 per cent, a disparity of 4.3 to 1. Finally, it should be stressed that the income distribution in Ruyigi was relatively uneven (6.7 to 1) in spite of the virtual absence of cash crops.

The gap between the average incomes per holding in Bubanza and Ngozi tends to disappear if the comparison is between incomes per person or per active worker, because of differences in family structure. On average, there were fewer people or active workers per family in Bubanza, as shown in Table 39.

The number of people per family was highest in Ngozi (4.71) and lowest in Bubanza (4.23). A slight difference between the figures for Ngozi and Ruyigi is explained by the overpopulation in Ngozi, which makes it difficult for the younger members to leave and set up elsewhere. The figure for Bubanza is appreciably lower because many of the families are young and with young children and have only recently settled in the peasant communities.

Table 39. **Agricultural income per person and per active worker,**
by region

In FBU

Region	Per person per year	Per active worker per day
Bubanza		
Gross income	7 627	
Net income	5 547	
Total net income	6 157	40.3
Ngozi		
Gross income	6 146	
Net income	5 752	
Total net income	5 895	39.6
Ruyigi		
Gross income	4 413	
Net income	4 076	
Total net income	4 170	26.9
Total		
Gross income	6 166	
Net income	5 475	
Total net income	5 776	36

As a result of these differences, net incomes per person, the most significant indicator of differences in the standard of living, were nearly the same in Bubanza and Ngozi (5 547 FBu and 5 752 FBu for net agricultural income, 6 157 and 5 895 for total net income) and exceeded those of Ruyigi by 40 or 44 per cent (net agricultural income or total net income). The average for the three regions together was about 5 500 FBu, or 60 dollars – 64 dollars, if one takes total net income (5 776 FBu). It is of interest to compare these figures, 60 and 64 dollars, with estimates of GNP per head. The World Bank gives for the same year a figure for GNP per head of 130 dollars[35], or roughly double. Two comments are needed, however. First, the World Bank figures are for GNP and not net national product; second, income per head in agriculture (excluding outside income) is always well below the national average – for example, 47 per cent of the national average in Senegal and Madagascar, where agriculture employs 75 to 80 per cent of the active population[36]. If allowance is made for these two adjustments, the figure of 60 dollars appears to be consistent with that of the World Bank.

The same differences can be seen in income per active worker. The figures for Bubanza and Ngozi were almost the same and 48 per cent higher than for Ruyigi. This means that whether one takes income per person or per active worker, the two regions with cash crops attained incomes 40 to 50 per cent higher than the basic income of the traditional subsistence economy.

Table 40. **Productivity per hectare of cultivated land,
by age of farmer and by region**

Age group of respondent	Percentages of respondents with values of production per hectare in the following ranges: (FBU)			Total	
	0-19 999	20 000-39 999	≥40 000	%	Number of respondents
Bubanza	68.9	24.2	6.9	100	563
≤20	91.7	8.3	0.0	100	12
21-40	64.1	28.3	7.6	100	237
41-60	70.0	23.0	7.0	100	257
≥61	78.9	15.8	5.3	100	57
Ngozi	47.3	30.3	22.4	100	505
≤20	0.0	0.0	100.0	100	2
21-40	45.9	28.1	26.0	100	242
41-60	50.5	32.8	16.7	100	204
≥61	43.9	31.6	24.6	100	57
Ruyigi	62.3	24.5	13.2	100	477
≤20	100.0	0.0	0.0	100	4
21-40	54.1	28.4	17.4	100	218
41-60	66.8	21.6	11.6	100	199
≥61	75.0	21.4	3.6	100	56
Total					
≤20	83.4	5.5	11.1	100	18
21-40	54.7	28.2	17.1	100	697
41-60	63.0	25.6	11.4	100	660
≥61	65.9	22.9	11.2	100	170

Finally, it is interesting to look at the evolution of income over a normal life-span in order to have an idea of the inequalities in total income received in a whole life and not in a single year. Table 40 shows the way in which land productivity varies in relation to the age of the farmer.

Two features characterise the effects of age. First, the effects are in general only slight, if one compares the average productivity of farmers in the 20-40 and over-60 age groups; and second, productivity decreases with age. This latter feature comes out clearly in Bubanza and Ruyigi: as age increased, the distribution between the three productivity groups altered, the percentage in the low-productivity group increasing and that of the high-productivity group declining. In Ngozi, the same was true up to 60 years of age, but the tendency was reversed for farmers over 60. This may be due to the over-population. In this region, but only here, the older farmers benefit from the help of younger members of the family who have been unable to set up on their own for lack of land, which would explain the closeness of productivity levels to those of the young farmers. Overall, the decline in productivity with age probably stems from the techniques used. Since mechanisation remains marginal for the majority of holdings, the gradual decline in physical strength necessarily affects the results obtained by the farmers. The relatively small extent of the variations has the important consequence that inequalities over a whole life-span are scarcely smaller than those for a single year for the farmers who comprise the largest group of active workers in Burundi. This is the reverse of the situation observed in the developed countries, where within the largest group, the wage-earners, the degree of inequality is substantially smaller for the whole life-span than for an individual year[37].

B.   Household Expenditure

The forecasts contained in development plans are valid only if the expenditure habits, patterns and levels of the various social groups are known with sufficient precision. In addition, the cost-of-living index is an indispensable indicator for measuring the economic situation, and this can only be calculated if enquiries have been made concerning consumption. And yet enquiries of this kind are practically non-existent in Burundi. Because of the costs and practical difficulties involved, the rare enquiries that have been made have concerned only certain population strata, or certain regions during a brief period.

Although the enquiry forming part of the present research was not principally intended as a specific study of household budgets, it nevertheless obtained useful information on the monetary expenditure of households, broken down between consumption goods and production inputs.

Table 41 brings out the structural differences between the average monetary expenditures in the three regions. Average expenditure per household is a statistic which facilitates inter-regional comparison. The table shows that average expenditure per household was 27 594 FBu in Bubanza, but as low as 7 610 FBu in Ngozi and 6 064 FBu in Ruyigi. The difference between a household living in the peasant communities in the Rusizi plain and one living in the interior was therefore of the order of four to one. This is largely because the peasant communities in the plain are to a great extent integrated into the market system, with a consequently greater degree of monetisation of the economy than in Ngozi or Ruyigi.

Table 41 distinguishes between household consumption expenditure and expenditure on production inputs. According to the information obtained, an average household devotes four-fifths of its monetary resources to consumption goods and one-fifth to production inputs.

Table 41. Average monetary expenditure by households, in FBU, on consumer goods and on production inputs in the three regions

	Bubanza		Ngozi		Ruyigi		Three regions	
	Average value	%	Average value	%	Average value	%	Average value	%
I. Consumption expenditure	21 942	100.0	6 472	100.0	4 847	100.0	11 761	100.0
1. Food *of which* :	14 539	66.2	3 063	47.4	2 310	47.7	7 124	60.6
Food crops	4 826	22.0	267	4.1	268	5.5	1 972	16.8
Meat	1 973	9.0	607	9.4	464	9.6	1 074	9.1
Fish	2 332	10.6	34	0.5	23	0.5	890	7.6
Beer	1 345	6.2	305	4.7	195	4.0	660	5.6
2. Clothing	3 400	15.5	1 735	26.8	1 353	27.9	2 241	19.0
3. Miscellaneous goods	2 896	13.2	1 290	19.9	939	19.4	1 784	15.2
4. Transport	571	2.6	90	1.4	83	1.7	268	2.3
5. Health	410	1.9	255	3.9	136	2.8	276	2.3
6. Education	126	0.6	39	0.6	26	0.5	68	0.6
II. Expenditure on production inputs	5 652		1 138		1 217		2 850	
III. Total expenditure	27 594	100.0	7 610	100.0	6 064	100.0	14 611	100.0
Consumption	21 942	79.5	6 472	85.0	4 847	79.9	11 761	80.5
Production inputs	5 652	20.5	1 138	15.0	1 217	20.1	2 850	19.5

The structure of household expenditure shown in Table 41 separates the main groups of products corresponding to the basic needs of the family. In all three regions, food is the largest item, accounting for two-thirds of the total in Bubanza, as against a little under half (47 per cent) in Ngozi and Ruyigi. Purchases of food crops come top of the household needs in the Rusizi plain, at one-third of total food expenditure, while in the two regions of the interior the share is less than 10 per cent. This difference reflects an essential difference between the two types of household: in Bubanza, they are already partly specialising in cash crops and have to buy in much of the food crops they consume, while in the other regions they produce enough food for their own family needs, regardless of whether they have developed cash crops or not.

It is interesting to note that food consumption habits in the Rusizi plain are different from those in the interior of the country: the plains household, because of the proximity of Lake Tanganyika, spends 16 per cent of its total food expenditure on fish, which is hardly consumed at all in Ngozi and Ruyigi.

Clothing comes second after food in the ranking of items of household consumption, accounting for 15 per cent of consumption expenditure in Bubanza, compared with 27 per cent in Ngozi and Ruyigi. Spending on miscellaneous items (batteries, paraffin, soap, tobacco, etc.) constitutes a fairly substantial part of the household budget: 19 per cent of consumption expenditure in Ngozi and Ruyigi, 13 per cent in Bubanza. Next comes expenditure on transport, health and education, still at a very low level.

To have a better picture, it is necessary to go beyond the average figures and look at the distribution of households according to their levels of expenditure, which in the end determines the real standard of living. Overall, the dispersion of consumption expenditure in Ngozi and Ruyigi is slight, with 85 to 90 per cent of households falling in the ranges between 1 000 FBu and 10 000 FBu (Table 42). The dispersion is even less marked for food spending (Table 43), by reason of its nature. On the other hand, dispersion is more pronounced in Bubanza, where the majority of households spend more than 15 000 FBu, whereas 30 per cent fall into the first two ranges (1 000 to 10 000 FBu).

The specificity of Bubanza shows the clear link between dispersion of expenditure and its average level. When expenditure rises sharply as a result of integration of households into the market economy and their agricultural specialisation, the increase in incomes is not evenly spread over the whole population. In practice, a substantial minority are left with low levels of income and expenditure, as in Ngozi and Ruyigi, while the majority achieve levels of spending which are three or four times higher. It would be erroneous, however, to draw the conclusion that regional differences in the standard of living are as great as this, because the figures take

Table 42. **Total annual monetary expenditure on consumption by households, by region**

Region	Percentages of households with annual expenditure on consumption in the following ranges (FBU)[1]					Total	
	0	1-4 999	5 000-9 999	10 000-14 999	≥15 000	%	Number of observations
Bubanza	0.3	9.5	20.1	15.3	54.8	100	591
Ngozi	0.8	50.5	34.2	9.6	4.9	100	512
Ruyigi	1.4	65.7	24.4	5.4	3.1	100	484
Total	0.8	39.9	26.0	10.4	22.9	100	1 587

1. Expenditure on food crops, clothing, miscellaneous goods (soap, batteries, etc.), transport, health, education.

Table 43. **Annual monetary expenditure by households on food, by region**

Region	Percentages of households with annual expenditure on food in the following ranges:[1] (FBU)						Total	
	0	1-1 999	2 000-3 999	4 000-5 999	6 000-7 999	≥8 000	%	Number of observations
Bubanza	0.3	7.6	14.2	11.3	8.5	58.1	100	591
Ngozi	1.4	52.7	24.6	11.1	4.7	5.5	100	512
Ruyigi	3.1	61.4	21.9	6.2	4.5	2.9	100	484
Total	1.5	38.6	19.9	9.7	6.0	24.3	100	1 587

1. Expenditure by households on food crops, meat, fish and beer.

no account of on-farm consumption, which represents a substantial part of total resources, the absolute value being much the same in all regions.

After the presentation of the basic data on household expenditure, it is desirable to see what economic or non-economic variables are likely to influence the expenditure behaviour of households.

The outward-looking nature of the household seems to play a decisive role, both because it corresponds to the availability of outside resources and because of the links with other variables (agricultural income, level of education, etc.) which have analogous effects. Thus, in cases where one or more members of a family had left to set themselves up on land in another region or to work in the town, the family spent much more on average than the others (5 805 FBu per adult against 3 842 FBu). Furthermore, households where one member had taken a job outside, but without leaving home, spent 9 662 FBu per person compared with 5 621 FBu for families where no member had an outside job. The same was true of farmers who took on wage-earners, either temporarily or permanently: their expenditure per person amounted to 7 212 FBu compared with 2 483 FBu for families where all the work of the farm was done by family members. These differences show that the integration of families into the market economy, on the demand side, is closely linked to the availability of the monetary resources on which the employment of outside labour depends and which, in turn, is increased by any outside activity on the part of a member of the family.

Expenditure per person also varied with the level of education of the head of household, this factor operating in combination with such social variables as religion or relations with the authorities. Where the farmer had had more than three years of primary school and, possibly, attended secondary school, expenditure per adult amounted to 5 484 FBu compared with 3 300 FBu and 3 400 FBu for those who were illiterate or had had only brief primary schooling. But there were marked variations within these groups depending on other variables. Among the illiterate farmers, the average expenditure was 2 636 FBu or 3 844 FBu, depending on whether the contacts with the commissioner were none or frequent. Similarly, among those with more than three years of primary school, the expenditure was 7 050 FBu in the case of those with frequent contacts, 5 375 FBu without them.

Religion also has an influence. For example, among the illiterate group, annual expenditure per person was 3 159 FBu for the Catholics, 3 607 for the pagans and 4 465 for the Protestants. The same difference could be seen in the group with long primary education: the average was 4 917 FBu for Catholics and 8 080 FBu for Protestants. There is therefore no support for the claim that it is the modern religions which have an effect, since for all levels of education the average expenditure of the pagans exceeded that of the Catholics. Belonging to

76

a Protestant church was important, on the other hand. These farmers presented a number of distinct characteristics: the average size of their holdings was larger; they devoted more land to cash crops (see Section II); they had higher levels of education (43 per cent having gone beyond three years of primary school, compared with 37 per cent of Catholics and 2 per cent of pagans). These characteristics taken together make them better prepared than other families for entry into the market economy.

For all the families, these social variables affected both the level of production of the farmers and their expenditure. For example, those who had frequent contacts with the authorities, who normally sold most of their production, who benefited from certain types of assistance, etc., had more monetary income and could spend more. It is therefore impossible to link expenditure with these variables without also placing expenditure in the context of the holding and taking into account all the variables affecting the way it is run.

CONCLUSION

This study has shown, or confirmed, two fundamental facts: first, that the development of agriculture can slow down the drift to the towns; second, that cash crops are an effective means of raising farmers' production and net income. The replies by parents show that the smaller the value of production, the more frequent is the desire that children move out of agriculture. At the same time, cash crops can be seen to pose no threat to food crops, since the region where there are no cash crops turns out to be the one with the lowest food production per active worker. In any case, where the crop concerned has a relatively high value, like coffee, the area devoted to it is small in relation to that under food crops. At the same time, comparison between Ngozi and Ruyigi shows that coffee increases the net income per active worker or per individual by 45 per cent compared with the subsistence economy holdings of Ruyigi. This result is obtained despite a shortage of land and unmodernised holdings. Admittedly, the impact of cash crops is less favourable in Bubanza, with income per household only 22 per cent higher than in Ruyigi and income per individual 34 per cent higher. But these mediocre results stem from the Government's price policy. If the prices for rice and cotton were to be doubled, for example, the differences would be 50 per cent and 60 per cent in Bubanza's favour. Furthermore, as will be shown, there are a number of measures which should be taken to increase production per active worker, concerning the equipment used, agricultural research, or information. It can be estimated that if these were applied, cash crops could lead to a substantial increase, even a doubling, of the farmers' net income. There seems to be no other strategy which, in the space of a few years and with relatively cheap investment, could bring about a doubling in the standard of living of the majority of the population in a poor country.

The measures recommended to reach this goal need to be described in some detail. Essentially they consist of: price rises for rice and cotton; the construction of roads; investment in traditional tools and small-scale agricultural equipment; agricultural research; improvement in the support and training given to farmers.

The first action to be taken should be to increase the prices of cotton and rice. It is quite unreasonable that rice should be bought from the farmer at a third of the price paid for it in Bujumbura, with a resultant monetary income per hectare lower than that obtained from sorghum or bananas. An increase of the order of 100 per cent for rice, and a substantially smaller one for cotton, should be introduced. Any attempt to promote these crops or any policy of external support is pointless if the prices paid to farmers are not remunerative. Conversely, farmers would certainly react to price increases by expanding the areas planted so that increases in production and in prices would combine to raise the farmers' incomes even more substantially.

Two of the measures concern investment. First, there must be an improvement in the road network in the regions remote from the capital, such as Ngozi and Ruyigi, where transport difficulties constitute a serious handicap for the marketing of agricultural produce. In addition, both the traditional farm implements (hoes, machetes, pruning knives, axes, picks) and light agricultural machinery should be made available at prices subsidised by the State. The profitability of these types of equipment is in fact very high: production per hectare in Ngozi doubles when the value of this equipment rises from 750 FBu per hectare to 1 800 FBu. Moreover, these implements are made in the country and are fairly cheap. In those regions where it is still possible to extend the area under cultivation, the labour force available within the family is often insufficient. In this case, some degree of mechanisation, in the form of light and rugged small-scale equipment (one- or two-horsepower machines), is indispensable. Some State help is essential here, for both acquisition and maintenance (servicing facilities, rapid import of spare parts).

Another recommendation is for a programme of agricultural research. The present impact on productivity of selected seeds, fertilizer, and anti-erosion practices turns out to be slight or non-existent. It is therefore essential to carry out research which can have a significant effect on production through new products, more suitable use of inputs, improved systems of cultivation (optimal combinations of seeds, fertilizer, etc.). This is all the more important in Burundi because of the high population density and the fact that in certain regions this has made fallowing impossible.

A research programme of this kind must be coupled with more effective action at the level of the farmers. The present system of outside support has admittedly had a favourable impact on productivity in Bubanza, but not in the other regions. Even this observation is somewhat uncertain because the simultaneous analysis of the religious and outside support factors shows that religion provides a more powerful explanation of the differences in productivity. Furthermore, the study has shown that education and information (radio, newspapers, contacts with the authorities) have a significant or even a major effect on productivity per hectare and on the return per holding or per wage-earner. This calls for a complete re-thinking of the policy of outside support, to place it in a broader context involving the individual actions of the development corporations (through extension services or otherwise), the spread of primary education and the forms it takes (programmes, teaching methods), the role of the media and their expansion (press, radio or, at a later stage, television). The re-thinking should thus be applied at three levels – technical, educational and cultural – to make the farmers' management methods more rational and to make them more receptive to innovation. Because of the role played by religion, it may be desirable to ask church leaders, members of religious orders and missionaries to play a consultative role in the reformulation of this policy.

It must be stressed that all the proposed measures are linked. There is no point in building roads, for example, or in improving outside support, if prices for cash crops are to be kept artificially low or if the lack of machinery keeps supply inelastic. These actions must therefore form part of an agricultural development plan which provides the necessary co-ordination between them and defines the order in which they are to be applied.

NOTES AND REFERENCES

1. The administrative and topographic cadastral plans were of some use in designing the samples used in the study; unfortunately, the former did not go beyond the level of the commune and the latter were imprecise and incomplete. The aerial photographs, by showing the location of rural settlements, gave a picture of the distribution of the population.

2. For example, the idea of effort was introduced by means of a pair of contradictory proverbs: "you don't get rich without effort" and "the courtier has always outdone the farmer". After an initial discussion, the interviewer asked: "What does being rich mean to you?" "What can you yourself do to improve your situation?" "Have you already in your own life made any exceptional efforts?".

3. One cannot ignore the fact that there were certain inadequacies in the data used for sampling, the statistics of the Interior Ministry in Bujumbura and those of the local administrations being sometimes incomplete.

4. The effective intensity equals:

$$\frac{\Sigma \quad \text{number of days of work on each crop}}{\text{Total available area}}$$

whereas the theoretical intensity corresponds to:

$$\frac{\Sigma \ (\text{number of permanent workers} \times 300) + \text{number of days of temporary labour}}{\text{Total available area.}}$$

5. In view of the reluctance of the farmers to express themselves on these subjects and their difficulty in doing so, all these questions were formulated indirectly.

6. Concerning the impact of the religious factor on economic and social behaviour, see also Section IV.

7. It is difficult to compare these figures with those obtained for Bubanza because of the special character of the holdings of the farmers in the rice-growing sector.

8. The cash crops grown in Bubanza provide only a small return to the farmers because of the prices imposed by the Government.

9. P. Leurquin, *L'étude du revenu indigène en milieu coutumier*, Pol. Sci. Afr. Centr. – IRSAC – 1956, no. 1.

10. Ministère du Plan, République du Burundi, Plan quinquennal de Développement économique et social du Burundi 1968-1970, p. 40.

11. Institut Rundi de Statistiques (IRUSTAT).

12. SEDES, *Enquête statistique agricole 1967 dans la région de Ngozi et Gitega*, Paris, 1969. SEDES, *Les régions de Muyinga, Ruyigi et du Mosso*, Paris, 1970.

13. B. Capecchi, *La culture du caféier et du théier au Burundi*, thèse de doctorat IIIe cycle présentée devant l'Université de Bordeaux III, 28 septembre 1976, p. 51.

14. Figures supplied to the IMF by the Burundi authorities.

15. Ministère du Plan, Département des études et statistiques; supplément au Bulletin Statistique n° 35, juin 1977 et Supplément au Bulletin Statistique n° 36, juillet 1977.

16. i.e. (per kg.): cassava, 4 FBu; beans, 20 FBu; sweet potatoes, 3 FBu; maize, 6 FBu; bananas, 5 FBu; sorghum, 20 FBu; potatoes, 14 FBu; groundnuts (unshelled, unroasted), 30 FBu. The price of a litre of beer was 10 FBu.

17. For rice, 20 FBu per kg.; coffee, 110 FBu per kg.; cotton (first quality), 30 FBu per kg. and 10 FBu per kg. for second quality.

18. 7 925, 9 533 and 7 215 FBu respectively for Bubanza, Ngozi and Ruyigi.

19. The Bubanza farmers are favoured by better roads, better health facilities and better schools, as well as by the availability of farm machinery, fertilizers and selected seeds and the technical support provided by agronomists and extension workers.

20. The Imbo is the natural geographic area consisting of the Rusizi plain and its extension along Lake Tanganyika.

21. A report by SRDI, the company responsible for promoting the growing of rice, acknowledges that bananas and sorghum earn more money per hectare than rice or cotton.

22. Productivity per unit of land is not, strictly speaking, the appropriate measure because it represents the gross value of production and not the net income. However, the analysis would be the same for net incomes, since the inputs required for food crops are no more costly than for cash crops.

23. i.e., the value of production per unit of labour minus expenditure on inputs other than land or labour.

24. As early as 1933, the Head of the Church in Burundi was strongly urging the missionaries to preach to the farmers the advantages of growing coffee, the only cash crop at the time.

25. This is partly the result of the intervention of the Catholic Church in the 1930s. The Church preached the gospel of cash crops to its faithful while the pagan traditionalists persisted with food crops. However, the present State extension service is available to all the farmers and affects the non-Catholics at least as much as the Catholics.

26. This is not necessarily the same thing as modern agriculture in a technical sense, because it may have very few capitalist characteristics and may preserve many traditional techniques. It will in fact then be a semi-traditional market agriculture.

27. It should be added that the most prosperous farmers, with the largest holdings, often choose to spend their money, not on investment, but rather for other purposes, notably ostentatious prestige consumption.

28. Cattle ownership appears to have an important impact on the level of savings. For the three regions, only 9.8 per cent of farmers owning no cattle had a level of savings exceeding 5 000 FBu, whereas 21.3 per cent of livestock producers with cattle worth more than 25 000 FBu reported this level of savings.

29. Cattle- and poultry-manure as well as compost.

30. For a better understanding of the effects of fallowing on soil productivity, it is necessary to allow for its duration, which can vary from one crop season to over two years. As the period lengthens, land productivity increases. Account must also be taken of the share of fallow in the land used. In theory, the higher this share, the greater the productivity of the cultivated land. This relationship is confirmed in the results for Ngozi and Ruyigi, but the reverse is true in Bubanza, where productivity falls as the share of fallow rises.

31. Including all farmers using selected seeds, whether for one or several food crops.

32. A similar significant relationship can be seen between ownership of cattle and contact with the authorities. For the three regions, those having no contact with the district commissioner were proportionately most numerous among farmers owning no cattle, while farmers with frequent contacts were relatively more numerous in the cattle-owning group.

33. Among the regions, Ruyigi is the one where fewest farmers had received any education: only one-third of the respondents had had any contact with school. At the other end of the scale, the proportion was highest in Ngozi, where half the population had attended school. The fact that Bubanza came only second may seem surprising (41.6 per cent of respondents) as it is close to the capital and already highly involved in the market economy. However, most of the farmers originate from the interior hill-districts and those who decided to leave their ancestral lands were usually the most disadvantaged. Nevertheless, this is the region where the highest proportion had reached secondary level, 4.6 per cent against 1.2 per cent in Ngozi, which proves the openness of the families to the idea of a modern educational system. The relatively high incidence of education of the Ngozi farmers, at least at primary level, may stem from the fact that the money earned from coffee makes it easier to allow children to attend school. The situation is the reverse in Ruyigi with its mainly subsistence economy, where the school remains far removed from social and economic reality. Fewer of the farmers interviewed in this region had attended school and these had left earlier than in the other regions.

34. This hypothetical calculation takes no account of any effects such a price increase would have on the volume of production. It is in fact likely that farmers would increase their production, at present held back by low profitability.

35. World Bank, *World Development Report*, 1979, page 126.

36. Data for:
   – Madagascar, taken from J. Lecaillon et D. Germidis, *Inégalité des revenus et développement économique*, Paris, PUF 1977, page 92.
   – Senegal, from C. Morrisson, *Income Distribution in Senegal*, 1976, World Bank (DRC).

37. Concerning this fall, see B.R. Schiller, *Relative earnings mobility in the United States*, A.E.R., December 1977, and L.A. Lillard, *Inequality: earnings vs. human wealth*, A.E.R., March 1977.

Part Two

METHODOLOGY:
THE METHOD USED TO ANALYSE
ECONOMIC AND SOCIAL CHANGE
IN A PEASANT SOCIETY IN CENTRAL AFRICA

*During the phase of conceptualisation leading up to the enquiry itself and to the analysis
of results, the author benefitted from the collaboration
of M. Primus Monn, lecturer in sociology at the University of Burundi.*

I. THE TECHNIQUES USED

Studies of rural life in the form of ethnological monographs exist in abundance. Unfortunately, they are fragmentary and limited in both time and space. Analysis of social change in the rural areas cannot be confined in this manner and requires an original approach.

In other words, the approach in this study was not adopted by chance but was deliberately chosen to accomplish a theoretical and at the same time practical objective, since the unearthing of fact constantly leads to questions concerning not only current practices but also current economic theory. That is where the economists tend to disagree. The factual evidence demands new forms of analysis and new research methods in both the advanced and the developing countries. There is no escaping the fact that there are as many types of economic psychology as there are schools of economic and social thought.

The realisation, in the light of the study of non-Western or pre-industrial social structures in rural areas, that economic rationality is not an absolute concept, combined with doubts about the value of rapid unilateral economic growth, oblige us sometimes to entertain serious doubts also about the value of economic theory itself. If the farmer from the hills of Burundi leaves the plainlands where the colonisers wanted to settle him and abandons his crops, there must be a reason, given that the way of life he has been offered is a "paradise".

What is needed is a clinical re-analysis of rural society using new tools, borrowed from a wide range of disciplines but in this case used for new purposes and in a broader perspective, without too much heed to inter-disciplinary boundaries. The method described and explained below is therefore a very wide-ranging one, needing a brief definition and justification.

Starting from an enquiry into the material aspects of the life of the Burundian farmer, the aim was to use the quantitative and qualitative data obtained in order to discern as precisely as possible his economic psychology, how he sees himself, what kind of farmer he would like to be or feels he ought to be, how he reacts to outside intrusion and to the changes in his relations with his own people as well as with outsiders. This list demonstrates the personal nature of the approach, since it aims at providing a picture of the individual, leaving enlightenment concerning the various groups to be derived indirectly and a posteriori.

In order to bring out clearly the basic parameters for a coherent rural development policy or to find a compromise or a basis for collaboration in the interests of overall development of the country which could narrow the differences between violently opposed social groups – presumably because of their unequal positions on the social and economic chessboard – would it not have been better to use some form of collective analysis in order to understand the dynamics of the various groups? Of course it would. But one must not put the cart before the horse.

There is no doubt that a study of the social dynamics involved (based on group dynamics), building initially on discussions within each group and, at a later stage, discussions between groups (farmers, officials, traders, expatriate experts, agronomists) would have allowed each of them to define their own interests and make their views known concerning social change. From there, it might have been possible to discern the key parameters for a sound development policy. But is this realistic? Does it not imply an unwitting adherence to the classical theories of Ricardo and Adam Smith, who believed that the private interests of individuals and the competition among them cannot fail to be in the interest of all, of the nation and of the "people"? But is it not self-evident that there must be conflict of interest in the race for wealth? Have we not arrived at a unanimous realisation that the complex mechanisms in the economy – complex because of the sheer diversity of the various combinations involved – are largely insentient, difficult to portray in a model, determined by a whole imaginary or symbolic system, and so in the end almost impossible to explain in clear terms? In short, things are decided on quite another level and it would be illusory to think that each of us knows exactly what he wants and how best to promote and improve his own well-being.

Fully aware of the complexities of the economic and social phenomena in rural African society, and even more aware of the limitations of the choice made and of the plan of work, but at the same time under pressure because of the vital importance of the question, we submit the following description of the methods used and the detailed account of the enquiry are submitted for reflection and criticism.

Socio-economic analysis in rural Africa runs into two related problems: first, that of the choice of theoretical model; second, of the research techniques to be used. In a word, it raises the question of relevance. Are the models and techniques developed in the West and capable of describing Western reality always valid, especially in Africa? Would it not be better to borrow some of the techniques and results of anthropology? In any case, a thorough monographic and ethnographic knowledge of the society concerned and an identification of its specific character are indispensable conditions for any sociological study. Such basic knowledge should permit an adequate formulation of the various working hypotheses.

But this is not enough, because the main objective of sociological research is not to formulate hypotheses but rather to confront the reality of the situation being studied with certain hypotheses, partly stemming from an anthropological approach, but also with certain well-established sociological approaches and theories. These hypotheses, which must be based on a theoretical model and have a well-defined conceptual framework, will then be accepted or rejected according to how well they fit the facts – facts obtained by classic sociological techniques.

The anthropological approach, moreover, has the advantage of allowing the hypotheses to be formulated to suit the native linguistic categories. Once this effort of formulation has been completed, the approach becomes profitable through the use of anthropology's specific techniques, notably participatory observation and interviews in depth. At this point in the research, the main problem is that of moving from the conceptual level to the factual. Which of the observed facts should be related to the concept selected and what happens to the many-sided facts which cannot be fitted into any precise concept? To take an example, the role of the hoe goes beyond the general concept of production because its significance is simultaneously symbolic, economic, religious, legal and political. However, in spite of efforts to adjust hypotheses and concepts, the theoretical model used remains Western in character. This is why all the techniques applied in the study and emerging from this theoretical model were appropriately re-worked to make them relevant and operational. We tried to understand the mechanisms of rural development in Burundi through the eyes of the Burundian farmer being observed. Account also had to be taken of the ideas of the other participating social groups directly concerned, including the groups in power, especially the senior officials in the Ministère de l'Agriculture et de l'Elevage and those in the Ministère du Plan, who are responsible for establishing the main lines of agricultural policy.

It is up to the people involved in rural development (and to the reader) to judge the success of the attempt to create, on the one hand, an appropriate theoretical model and a conceptual framework to fit the social realities involved and, on the other, techniques to suit both the theoretical model and the observed facts.

Taken in order, the following techniques and methods of enquiry were chosen for the analysis of rural structure in Burundi and the way in which it is changing:
- preliminary documentation
- field observations and semi-directive in-depth interviews
- sampling method
- pilot enquiry and enquiry by means of questionnaires
- fieldwork
- processing of the data obtained.

A. Documentation

A whole series of existing documents, most of which had previously been little exploited by ethnologists and anthropologists, was methodically examined. Given the approach to be used in the research, the documentation sought had to be related to two main themes: social change and agricultural development. With this in mind, the documents which were considered to be significant could be grouped into four categories:
- Documents concerning the physical background (maps and aerial photographs); these documents were an essential tool for the sampling process. Existing aerial photographs gave an idea of the distribution of population and of housing settlements as seen in the natural surroundings. More detailed examination can give interesting indications of the distribution of crops and thus make it possible to draw up certain typologies in this respect. It is also possible with the help of these documents to make a first estimate of the areas cultivated or lying fallow. These aerial photographs cover only part of the territory, however. The available maps can be divided into four main types: educational (physical, economic, historical), tourist and road maps, administrative maps and topographic cadastral maps. Only the last two types were of any interest for the sampling method used in the study. The cadastral maps are on a scale

which would have been useful for sampling but were too imprecise and incomplete. The administrative maps do not go further than district level, which seriously reduces their value.

- Demographic documents: although somewhat imprecise, demographic data are available from the Population Division of the Ministère de l'Intérieur. The data for calculating population densities exist only for regions and districts, which means that it is impossible to calculate the densities for smaller units or hill-districts.

- Ethnological and anthropological documents: most of these date from the German and Belgian colonial periods, and so great care was needed in interpreting and weighing the information they contained. They could nevertheless provide useful information concerning economic, social, political and cultural organisation in the pre-colonial period. The information on farming and cattle-raising practices was of the greatest interest for the study of rural structures in present-day Burundi, as was the anthropological detail in the documents concerning Kirundi, the language of the country. (Expressing theoretical concepts using the native language as the vehicle makes it possible to take the epistemological step from research hypothesis to objective scientific observation.) It was the dictionaries and the collections of sayings and proverbs which above all helped the application of the concepts to actual research.

- Technical reports by agronomists and economists. These documents, produced either by the Belgian colonial administration or by bilateral or multilateral experts, are concerned essentially with cash crops (coffee, cotton and tea), with the problems of food crops taking second place. These reports give useful and precise indications on the relationship between labour input (per day) and the crops harvested, in the form of numerical data related to the number of hectares of cultivated land, etc.; they also contain valuable information on the farming calendar, farming techniques, the nature of the soil and its fertility, the overall importance of various crops, the marketing of produce, the breakdown of farmers' expenditures, etc. However, they deal almost exclusively with the peasant communities and with projects financed by external aid and do not touch on the traditional peasant agriculture.

B. Observation and semi-directive in-depth interviews

It is not easy for a Western researcher to enter the world of the African peasant with its totally different values, reasoning and logic. It is still less easy to transpose the theoretical model and conceptual framework into actual research activities. The ideal solution of this difficulty would have been to use the technique of participatory observation, which requires that the researcher must himself become part of the milieu being studied. However, this would have implied complete familiarity with Rundi language and culture, obtainable only after years of preparation, the traditional Kirundi language being regarded as particularly abstruse and difficult to acquire, particularly because of its wealth of subtle proverbs, whose significance is sometimes missed even by Barundi if they have lost touch with their roots.

In order to put them within reach of the population being examined, the research concepts were transposed into the traditional proverbs familiar to the farmers. The proverbs chosen, dealing with a limited number of subjects, had to fit the theoretical framework of the research. Some of these subjects held a greater significance for the traditional society – although they could also indicate the degree of movement away from that society –such as the hoe, the cow, the dowry, the idea of god, authority, disease; others were more meaningful

84

for modern society – but also existed in traditional society – such as work, the value of money, conflicts,the problem of justice, migration, the meaning of effort, ambitions to leave farming. To keep the respondents as free as possible from influence on the part of the interviewers, contradictory proverbs on the various chosen subjects were thrown into the discussion, either simultaneously or at different stages of the interview, and left open for free debate by the farmers. This method was intended to rid them of any tendency they might have to distort the truth in a desire to conform socially or any wish they might have to improve their standing in the eyes of the interviewers (students or European professors)[1].

As an illustration, the subject of migration was tackled partly by using the two following proverbs: "Akanyoni katagurutse ntikamenya iyo bweze", meaning "a bird which doesn't fly doesn't know where the ripe seeds are"; and "Akaguru karekare gata nyeneko mumahwa", meaning "those with long legs fall into the thorns." In other words, the first proverb implies that in order to survive it is necessary to move about, to seek a living elsewhere and leave one's traditional background, while the second is a warning of the unfavourable consequences of moving, of abandoning tradition or indeed of any form of change. Another example, this time concerning the meaning of effort, was the pair of proverbs "nta wutunga atagowe" ("you don't get rich without effort") and "nzisabira yaruse nzirimira" ("the courtier has always done better than the farmer"). The first one affirms that only hard work will allow the farmer to improve his situation, while the second implies that social situation and status, rather than individual effort, are what decide one's material well-being.

For each pair of contradictory proverbs the farmers covered by the qualitative enquiry had all the time they needed to express themselves freely and spontaneously, in a conversation taking place in a cordial atmosphere over the traditional jar of beer. When the farmer had had his say, some significant elements of the proverb with particular relevance to the research were thrown back into the discussion and taken further through a series of open questions with the aim of understanding the real-life experiences of the respondents.

For example, once the farmer had spoken freely on "you don't get rich without effort", the main elements of the proverb were approached through the following questions: "what does 'being rich' mean to you?" (attitudinal question: the meaning of wealth); "what can you yourself do to improve your situation?" (attitudinal question: the farmer's perception of the possibilities of changing his condition); "have you already in your own life made any exceptional efforts?" (factual question: the farmer's personal experience concerning effort). When this part of the interview was over, the contrary proverb was not always introduced immediately, to prevent the statement and replies about the first proverb blocking discussion on the meaning to be given to the contradictory one. For example, on the subject of effort, a break was made by introducing a new subject – in this case, the willingness to take risks. For this purpose, the proverb "urima aziganya yimbura bike" (sow only part of your seed and your harvest will be small) was put forward for consideration. Once this diversionary subject had been exhausted, the contradictory proverb "the courtier has always done better than the farmer", explored more deeply by means of questions, supplied the theme for the next stage of the discussion.

These qualitative interviews were carried out with the help of interpreter-interviewers who had been given strict training and who were chosen from people living in rural areas and able to gain the confidence of the farmers. The type of approach used required that the interpreter-interviewer be socially close to the farmers in mentality and behaviour. In addition he had to have a lively mind and be capable of thinking in sufficiently abstract terms to understand the ideas underlying the study. The quality of these interpreter-interviewers was crucial to the success of the enquiry. The principal interpreter-interviewer, who had these necessary qualities although his education had hardly gone beyond the first years of secondary

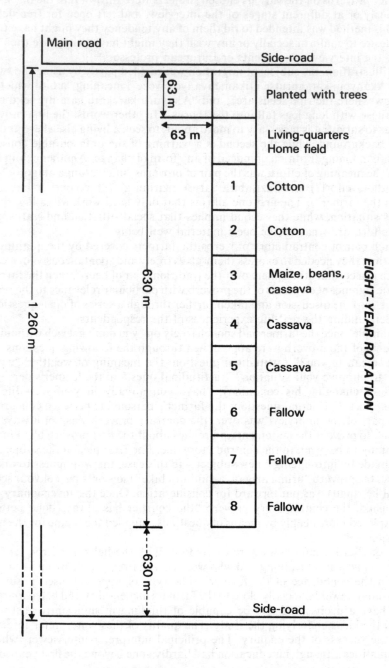

Figure 1
**THE STRIP-HOLDINGS OF PEASANT COMMUNITIES
IN THE RUSIZI**

Main road

Side-road

63 m

63 m

Planted with trees

Living-quarters
Home field

630 m

1 260 m

1 Cotton

2 Cotton

3 Maize, beans,
cassava

4 Cassava

5 Cassava

6 Fallow

7 Fallow

8 Fallow

EIGHT-YEAR ROTATION

630 m

Side-road

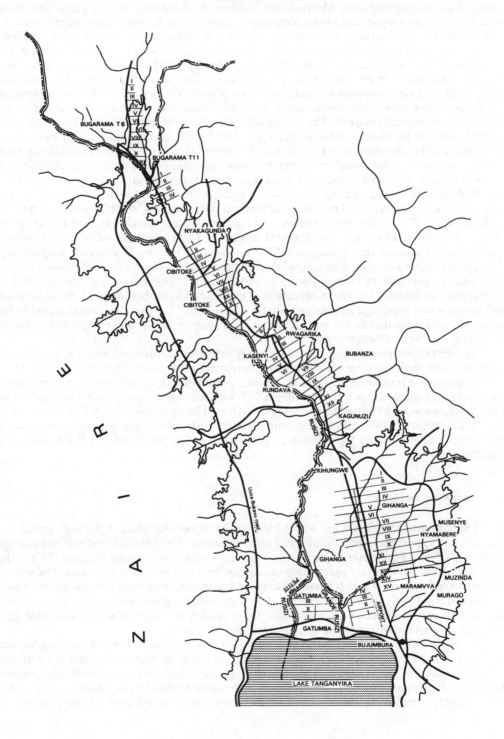

school, was a young Murundi. Married with children, he lived on a banana plantation in the interior of the country in conditions identical to those of the farmers being interviewed. In addition to his main activity as secretary of a rural dispensary, he also did some farming.

The meetings with the farmers were carried out according to the traditional etiquette. We made known our wish to have a discussion about the local proverbs and at the same time asked to know when the farmers would be available outside their normal activities. The interview itself, fixed for a time proposed by the farmer, took place in the rugo, the family compound, or sometimes even inside the respondent's hut. The interview opened with certain ritual expressions of mutual goodwill. The farmer spread mats at the entrance to the main hut and offered stools to his visitors, who in return presented a jug of beer made from bananas or sorghum. Unlike an interview in Europe, which usually takes place between individuals, each of these interviews, even though it started with just the head of the rugo soon developed into a collective affair, with close or less close neighbours and passers-by, attracted by the beer or the sound of conversation, gathering in increasing numbers to join in the discussion, which was then kept constantly in play. The interest of this method is obvious, since it involves groupings of individuals. The replies then take on a sociological value, simply because the situation obliges those present to reach some degree of consensus. Each interview, recorded on tape, was transcribed, translated into French and finally submitted to content analysis. Surprisingly, the farmers showed only mild distrust of the tape-recorders. Where these did cause a serious problem, the preliminary conversation was played back to them, and this was sufficient to re-establish confidence. In order to obtain their collaboration or their interest, the request for an interview was presented as coming from the University, "the most important school in the country", which wanted to know more about their way of life in order to provide a better education for their children.

The first experimental stage, carried out only in the Rusizi plain, was limited to about ten semi-directive in-depth interviews, with the participation of about thirty people. The job of transcription and translation of these interviews, performed at the university, was given to a student from a country area who was still in touch with his own milieu. To avoid any distortion, the recordings were submitted to a second translation. The resulting texts, full of information, were then compared and analysed for content. The results of this analysis were then used in making the most suitable formulation of the questionnaire to be used in the quantitative analysis.

C. Sampling methods

The sampling techniques are determined by the theoretical aims of the study, involving two possible approaches: longitudinal and cross-sectional. The first of these portrays change by means of prolonged observation of social groups – sometimes lasting decades. This is the ideal approach, but is rarely practicable because of financial or time constraints. The second was preferred because it avoids these limitations. It consists of analysing social groups which are each at a different stage of the process of change, with the constraints on change being felt in different ways in each. This cross-sectional approach has certain major disadvantages, however, in particular, problems of comparability of data.

Given the difficulties related to this approach, three regions were chosen, each quite different from the two others, each subject to different forces of change and each at a different stage of transformation. These were the Rusizi plain, the Ngozi region and the Ruyigi region[2]. Ngozi and Ruyigi correspond to the provinces of the same names, but the plain is a geographic area roughly comprising the province of Bubanza and a small part of the province of

Bujumbura. The process of change is furthest advanced in the Rusizi plain. Here, the agricultural structure was more radically altered by Belgian colonisation than in any other part of the country. Land use was planned entirely around the development of cotton as a cash crop. Divided by a grid-pattern of longitudinal roads and side-roads into large geometric areas occupied by the peasant communities, each consisting of a number of small farms placed side-by-side, the whole region is made up of long strips of land, each 630 metres by 63 metres and divided into ten identical plots of 63 metres by 63 (Figure 1). The plot nearest the side-road has trees planted on it, the next has the house, two more are compulsorily devoted to cotton, while three of the others can be planted with food crops (maize, cassava, sweet potatoes, beans) or other crops; the last three are left fallow. Cotton-based crop rotation with an eight-year cycle is applied uniformly on all the farms in a given block. This facilitates supervision and extension work as well as crop-spraying of insecticides from the air. Since independence, however, there have been serious breaches in this organisation; many farmers no longer respect the discipline formerly imposed by the colonial power. What lies behind this "degradation", this slackening of farming discipline? Why are some of the peasant communities in the plain even being abandoned, and why is all this happening despite the existence of apparently ideal infrastructure and support (roads, irrigation channels, guidance from agronomists, dispensaries, schools, etc.)? To find and understand the answers to these questions it was important to place the facts in a wider context, including the regions of origin of those farmers least affected by this change.

In the interior of the country, agriculture has remained traditional, except for the effects of the high population density in Ngozi. Population pressure in this region is very strong: density here being by far the highest in the whole country (263 inhabitants per square kilometre in 1975 for the region as a whole and even exceeding 350 inhabitants per square kilometre in the Mwumba commune). This brings strong pressure for change, although the region is still essentially traditionalist. The situation in Ruyigi is quite different, with virtually no pressure for change, because it has the lowest population density in the country and abundant reserves of uncultivated land, quite sufficient for today's or tomorrow's farmers.

In Ngozi, the transformation process might be triggered either by more intensive agricultural production, by emigration to land available elsewhere, by giving up agriculture in favour of industrial or urban activities, or, finally, by reducing the number of births.

In Ngozi and Ruyigi, the sampling took place first at the commune level, then at the level of hill-districts[3] and finally by choosing the inhabitants within each of the hill-districts

Table 44. **Population density of communes in the Ruyigi region (1975) showing the communes chosen for the enquiry**

Communes in Ruyigi province	Population per sq. km.	Communes chosen
Kinyinya	31	Kinyinya
Cankuzo	34	
Mpinga	35	
Gisagara	36	
Bweru	55	Bweru
Nyabitare	55	
Ruyigi	61	Ruyigi
Rutana	99	Rutana
Butaganzwa	103	
Musongati	115	Musongati

Statistics provided by the Direction de la Population, Ministère de l'Intérieur.

selected. The sampling method used in the plain was different, given that in this region the enquiry concerned only the peasant communities and not the totality of holdings. The communes were chosen on the basis of population density. Five communes in each region were selected as follows: first, the two communes with the highest and lowest densities, respectively, then the commune with median density, and finally the two communes with densities between the two extremes and the median. As illustration, Table 44 shows how the Ruyigi communes were chosen.

Within each commune selected in Ngozi and Ruyigi, five hill-districts were drawn by means of systematic random sampling. The first was found by using the random numbers table of M.G.Kendall and Babington Smith. The remainder were then obtained by arithmetic progression, taking every third, fourth or fifth commune after the first, the exact interval depending on the total number of hill-districts in the commune. Table 45 shows, for illustration, the method for selecting the five hill-districts out of the 24 in the Musungati commune.

Table 45. **Complete list of hill-districts in the Musongati commune of the Ruyigi region, showing the hill-districts chosen for the enquiry**

Hill-districts	Hill-districts chosen	Method of choice
Buhinga		
Kamaramagambo		
Nyabigozi		
Nyabisindu	Nyabisindu	First to be drawn using random
Maganahe-Runyoni		numbers table
Maganahe-Gihera		
Yove		
Katagazi		
Rusunu	Rusunu	Second to be drawn in rotation
Kagunga		(every 5th)
Shanga		
Nyanza		
Mabawe		
Kisasa	Kisasa	Third
Nyakabanda		
Mbuza		
Nyangozi		
Karera		
Ngoma	Ngoma	Fourth
Nyabibuye		
Mwagara		
Mungwa		
Makakwe		
Chero	Chero	Fifth

List of hill-districts provided by the Ministère de l'Intérieur.

In each hill-district selected, the people to be interviewed were chosen in the same way as the hill-districts, using the files or registers of heads of household kept for each hill-district by the authorities of the commune or the zone. Only adult heads of household (practically all of them men) were considered.

For the communes, the sampling was carried out according to the numbers of adult males and the same method was used to decide the number of people to be interviewed in each hill-district. Convocations were sent to more farmers in each hill-district than the number derived by the sampling method or the number finally interviewed. At the very start of the quantitative enquiry in the field, the interviewers found that the people chosen by the sampling method were not always all present at the meeting-place. These absences, usually only few in number, resulted either from inaccuracies in the local authority's registers of heads of household, which sometimes included people who had died or migrated, or from illness or absence from the hill-district. This explains why the numbers on the interviewers' lists were always greater than the numbers set by the sampling method, in order to have some names in reserve to replace possible gaps. It even happened in some cases that the research group found themselves confronted at the meeting-place by several hundred people, including ten or so of the people actually selected, although only 20 or 30 farmers were actually needed for interview. This situation arose because the instructions from the communal administration had either been incorrectly passed on or had been misunderstood by the councillor who, instead of inviting the people selected for interview, had thought he was doing the right thing by bringing together the whole population of the hill-district. In such circumstances, the research group came back again later – as often as four times in some cases – so that the enquiry could be carried out in accordance with the criteria laid down by the research plan. In Africa, fieldwork is always full of surprises, however many precautions the researcher may take. It is up to him to face up to any unpredictable situations – and to all the quirks which give spice to empirical research in the field.

The number of people to be interviewed in each region was set at 500, in order to be able to use multivariate analysis when processing the results. This is the minimum figure for multivariate analysis at regional level. The simultaneous analysis of three variables each with three possible values means a theoretical average frequency of less than 20 observations per cell, and fewer still when there are gaps in the data or, a fortiori, in the case of sub-groups like coffee-producers or farmers growing only food crops. It should be stressed that the sample number was not chosen in relation to the population of the regions – 500 respondents account for 10 per cent of the adult males in the Bubanza plain and in Ruyigi, but only 4 per cent in Ngozi – but for the requirements of multivariate analysis at regional level.

Tables 46 and 47 show the existence of major differences between the numbers of adult males recorded by the Ministère de l'Intérieur in Bujumbura and those obtained from the registers and files – rarely kept up to date – of the communal authorities in the interior of the country. It is true that the coverage of the two sets of figures is not quite identical. The statistics of the Ministère de l'Intérieur are for adult males aged 18 or over, while those of the communes are for heads of household. Logically, the heads of household should be fewer in number than the males aged over 18. In practice, the differences work both ways. The communal statistics were preferred to those of the Ministère de l'Intérieur for the establishment of the sample, because they are based on actual lists of names.

It should also be noted that the number of people interviewed in each region is higher than the initially planned figure of 500. This is not accidental, but is due to the fact that it was necessary to plan for the likelihood that a certain number of questionnaires would be unusable. The total number of people interviewed was therefore 1 655, and the number of questionnaires finally used 1 588: 591 from Bubanza, 512 from Ngozi and 485 from Ruyigi.

The sampling method used in Bubanza had to be different, because the enquiry was to involve only the population living in peasant communities in the Rusizi plain. To design the sample, it was first necessary to know the population of these peasant communities. These figures were not available from the authorities, because their information related to the

91

Table 46. **The Ngozi sample**

Communes	Hill-districts	Males over 18[1]	Heads of household[2]	Sample Before enquiry	Sample Adjusted on the spot
Kiremba		1 020	638	119	110
	Bunogera	120	72	14	
	Gitaro	345	300	40	
	Kivoga	198	120	23	
	Musasa	100	58	12	
	Ruvumu	257	88	30	
Marangara		1 090	1 028	79	92
	Carwa	181	167	13	
	Gicumbi	196	194	14	
	Kigoma	205	204	15	
	Nduhwe	222	206	16	
	Ragwe	286	257	21	
Mwumba		1 313	944	76	79
	Burenza	216	257	13	
	Cahi	328	210	19	
	Kabatama	202	40	12	
	Kibindi	215	200	12	
	Rukurazo	352	237	20	
Rango		1 798	1 836	115	114
	Butanyerera	225	278	15	
	Gipfuvya	344	385	22	
	Kiguruka	286	315	18	
	Nyabiyogi	343	415	22	
	Rubungu	600	443	38	
Ruhororo		2 094	1 629	111	117
	Gitamo	526	208	28	
	Kabuye	333	291	18	
	Kobero	371	349	20	
	Nyakibingo	539	619	28	
	Rwamiko	325	162	17	
Total				500	512

1. Statistics provided by the Ministère de l'Intérieur.
2. Statistics from the registers of the communal administration.

hill-district administrative units whose boundaries go beyond those of the peasant communities. A special census therefore had to be made. For the peasant communities involved in regional development projects supported by outside assistance there were accurate statistics, but for the others a systematic census of heads of household was undertaken before the enquiry itself. The starting-point was a preliminary sample based on fragmentary information obtained from the documents of the COGERCO, the ISABU, the communal registers and various geographic maps of the plain. The census of the heads of household took place a few days before the main study and proceeded at the same pace. It was organised for each side-road with the help of the local administration and in most cases carried out by the farmers themselves The definitive sample was established as soon as the combined operations of the census and the first visit by the interviewers to the whole of the peasant communities had been completed. Once this sample was available, a supplementary enquiry was used to correct the initial sample in the light of more precise data from the census. This meant that in the definitive sample, the number of people interviewed for each side-road was in direct proportion to its importance in the total population of heads of household for the peasant communities as a whole.

Table 47. **The Ruyigi sample**

Communes	Hill-districts	Males over 18[1]	Heads of household[2]	Sample	
				Before enquiry	Adjusted on the spot
Bweru		768	736	121	110
	Busuma	196	187	31	
	Kanisha	109	119	17	
	Mubavu	138	138	22	
	Ntunda	218	202	34	
	Rutegama	107	90	17	
Kinyinya		443	511	68	79
	Bihembe	99	51	15	
	Kinyinya	109	331	17	
	Murehe	90	51	14	
	Nyakiyonga	80	44	12	
	Rusange	65	34	10	
Musongati		777	718	95	101
	Nyabisindu	178	195	22	
	Rusunu	82	189	10	
	Kisasa	190	150	23	
	Ngoma	190	118	23	
	Kobero	137	66	17	
Rutana		840	1 015	105	99
	Rongero	224	491	28	
	Rushemeza	145	142	18	
	Nyanzuki	108	88	14	
	Kivoga	154	142	19	
	Nyamure	209	152	26	
Ruyigi		956		111	95
	Kigamba	248	270	29	
	Migege	201	225	23	
	Nkongwe	150		17	
	Rugoti	198	177	23	
	Solero	159	194	19	
Total				500	484

1. Statistics provided by the Ministère de l'Intérieur.
2. Statistics from the registers of the communal administration.

Table 48. The Rusizi Plain Sample

Communes	Peasant communities: P or Villages: V		Side-roads	Heads of household, as counted		Final sample (decided on the spot)	
						Before enquiry	Adjusted during enquiry
Rugombo				1 820		125	121
	Rukama	P		591		42	
			1		151	10	
			2		142	12	
			3		115	10	
			4 A		90	6	
			4 B		93	4	
	North Imbo Project	P		694		42	
			1 A		87	6	
			2 A		77	4	
			3 A		146	6	
			4 A		133	9	
			1 B		33	4	
			2 B		31	3	
			3 B		59	4	
			4 B		43	2	
			5 B		45	2	
			Main road		40	2	
	South Imbo Project	P		535		41	
			5 A		82	6	
			6 A		82	6	
			6 B		46	3	
			7 A		61	7	
			8 A & B		30	3	
			9 A, B & C		66	4	
			10 A, B & C		80	8	
			11 A, B & C		66	4	
			12 B		22	–	
Buganda				2 010		130	129
	Murambi	P		87		5	
			1		35	2	
			2		52	3	
	Ruhagarika	P		348		25	
			1		133	8	
			2		215	17	
	Kasenyi	P		873		55	
			1		40	2	
			2		94	6	
			3		109	7	
			4		276	18	
			5		168	10	
			6		130	8	
			7		47	3	
			8		9	1	
	Ndava	P		381		23	
			1		17	1	
			2		35	2	
			3		113	7	
			4		91	5	
			5 & 6		125	8	
	Kagunuzi	P		321		22	
			1		35	2	
			2		74	4	
			3		77	6	
			4		75	4	
			5		41	4	
			6		19	2	

Table 48. *(cont.)* **The Rusizi Plain sample**

Communes	Peasant communities: or Villages:	P V	Side-roads	Heads of household as counted	Final sample (decided on the spot)	
					Before enquiry	Adjusted during enquiry
Mpanda				5 170	237	227
	Gihanga	P		1 120	68	
			1	80	4	
			2	131	8	
			3	154	10	
			4	85	6	
			5	59	4	
			6	64	4	
			7	44	2	
			8	52	4	
			Main road East and West	196	12	
			9	–	–	
			10	51	3	
			11	120	6	
			12	84	5	
				2 240	120	
	Bulamata	V		340	18	
	Muliza	V		400	22	
	Nyoshanga	V		710	36	
	Ninga	V		370	20	
	Mpanda	V		420	24	
	Nyamabere	P		1 810	49	
			7	87	5	
			8	107	7	
			9	183	11	
			10	176	11	
			11	137	8	
			12 North	108	7	
Mutimbuzi				1 810	111	112
	Kinekura	P		245	15	
			12 South	66	4	
			13	101	6	
			14	67	4	
			15	11	1	
	Maramvya	P		389	24	
			12	46	2	
			13	137	8	
			14	114	8	
			15	85	4	
			16	7	2	
	Muruka-ramu	P		521	32	
			1	42	4	
			2	106	6	
			3	162	10	
			4	174	10	
			5	37	2	
				263	16	
	Buhinyuza	V		128	8	
	Rubirizi	V		95	6	
	Mutakura	V		40	2	
	Gatumba	P		392	24	
			1	148	9	
			2	123	8	
			3	121	7	
Total				10 810[1]	603	591[2]

1. Data obtained from the census carried out for the purposes of the enquiry using documents from various development projects (Imbo Project, SRDI, COGERCO, ISABU).
2. Including two other people interviewed from unidentified communes.

95

Figure 2

ROTATION OF PEOPLE TO BE INTERVIEWED IN A RUGO
CONSISTING OF THREE HOUSEHOLDS

	1	2	3	4	5	6	7	8	9	10	11	12	13	14	15
Household of head of rugo	●						●			●	●	●			
Household of son		●			●				●				●		
Household of grandson			●	●		●		●						●	●

It should also be mentioned that a system of rotation of the individuals to be interviewed within a given rugo was drawn up with the help of random number tables, to ensure that where there were a number of heads of household in a rugo, each of them had the same chance of appearing in the sample. The aim was to prevent the enquiry from dealing only with the oldest heads of household in each rugo. Figure 2 shows how the interviewer had to approach a rugo consisting of three households: those of the head , his son and his grandson.

In rugos of this pattern, the interviewer would first interview the head of the rugo, the second time his son, the third and fourth times the grandson, the fifth time the son, and so on. Although the technique of rotating the people interviewed within a multi-household rugo was operationally possible, it was not applied because the administration's files and registers included not only the heads of rugo but all the heads of household, who were therefore all liable to be picked in the sample.

This being said, some reservations must be expressed about the data used for the sampling and about the sampling procedure itself. First, the data: the inconsistencies between the statistics of the Ministère de l'Intérieur available in the capital and those of the communal administrations in the interior of the country have already been mentioned. For one thing, they are not strictly comparable, the ones referring to adult males over 18 years of age, the others to heads of household without any indication of age. For another, statistics from both sources are sometimes incomplete and have obvious gaps. As for the sampling procedure, its design clearly depends on the approach used in the study. A country-wide sample, however, would have provided more valuable results on the rural structure in Burundi. Two remarks should be made here about the requirements imposed by the study. The first is a justification of the procedure in the sense that the aim was to observe different stages of the process of change, implying the need to select examples which were particularly significant from this specific point of view. The second is to note the technical and financial restrictions on the available resources which prevented the research from being carried out on a larger and more representative scale.

II.   THE PILOT ENQUIRY AND THE QUESTIONNAIRE

The final questionnaire used in the enquiry, in French and Kirundi, may be obtained from the Development Centre of the OECD

For efficient scientific observation of the farming milieu, it was necessary to pick out the most revealing elements for inclusion in the initial model and then proceed to a more thorough exploration of their meaning and content. Qualitative, in-depth interviews of a semi-directive nature, using proverbs, provided the link between the concepts and the quantitative observation. This anthropological approach permitted specification of certain qualitative features of the concepts and the identification of certain indicators as the most eloquent variables for a questionnaire to be arranged in the form of grouped questions. Out of the rich harvest obtained from the enquiry, the following qualitative features clearly stood out: education or the educational aspirations of the parents for their children, power relationships in the form of social justice, social mobility in the form of propensity to become involved in commercial activities, dominance of pre-capitalist forms of production as shown by the low importance attached to money and cash crops, value attached to food crops as a means of subsistence, complementarity between different types of crop, division of labour within the family, social organisation of work, technical organisation of production, and hierarchy of types of expenditure as an index of social change.

The questionnaire was drafted in two stages. A first version was submitted to the comments of knowledgeable Barundi, familiar with agricultural life, cultivation practices and cattle-raising techniques. Their criticisms and views had a positive impact on the preparation of the first document used in the enquiry. The resulting 540-question questionnaire was then submitted to a preliminary test in each of the three regions. This pilot enquiry covered about 15 farmers in each region. Once the results had been analysed, the definitive version of the questionnaire was drawn up.

The wide scope of the first questionnaire was due to the need to use the pilot enquiry to try out the largest possible number of questions in order to select the most significant indicators, in other words those which most clearly distinguished between the sociologically significant sub-groups. This pilot enquiry purposely aimed at choosing from the numerous indicators those showing the highest degree of reliability and validity. Some questions which turned out to have no discriminatory value – particularly concerning religious and political socialisation – were dropped because the answers obtained were virtually identical. The modifications made to the initial questionnaire also included a refinement of the method used to obtain information on agricultural production and farming activities.

A.   Farming activities

It is well known that the rhythm of the economic and social life of the farmer is seasonal, being especially associated with crop cycles. The first of these seasons runs from the beginning of September to the end of January, the second from February to June, and the third consists of July and August. The first two correspond to the rainy seasons and the third approximately to the dry season. To make the process of recall easier for the farmer, questions concerning production, consumption, sales and expenditure were arranged to fit the farming calendar, and then asked in four stages, starting with the present and working backwards. The first question – designed as a control and a bench-mark – concerned the four weeks preceding the enquiry; the second dealt with the most recent crop cycle (February to June), the one freshest in the memory because the enquiry started in July; the third, with the cycle before that (September to January) and the fourth, with the dry season of July and August of the previous year. Similarly, questions about different forms of agricultural work – in the case of food crops, preparation of the fields (tilling, manuring), sowing, weeding, harvesting – were put to each individual engaged in each category of work, distinguishing between members of the family and outsiders and between adults and children.

B.   The completion of the questionnaire

The pilot enquiry also made it possible to test the time taken over the questionnaire process and to work out the critical point at which fatigue prevented any further effective contribution from the farmer. The initial questionnaire usually took between four and six hours, depending on the activities of the respondent, the size of the family and the number of outside workers.

It was surprising to see the interest shown by the farmers in the questions. Their endurance and willingness lived up to all expectations: the interviews in the pilot enquiry were never once broken off. Signs of fatigue or weariness sometimes appeared after about the fifth hour. In explanation, mention was made of the need to pay a visit to friends, or to see neighbours or relations laid up in the dispensary. The interviewer was asked if the conversation could be completed with the other members of the family present. The reduction of the questionnaire to 395 questions got over this disadvantage. In normal practice, the respondents answered only about 200 questions, because of numerous optional paths the questioning could take and because some sets of questions were not relevant to every farmer interviewed. The time taken over the definitive questionnaire varied from case to case and from region to region, but was usually between an hour and a half and three hours.

C.   The structure of the final questionnaire

Although major modifications were made to the initial questionnaire, the structure in the final version remained more or less unchanged. The breakdown of the farmer's monetary expenditure, a question which had been raised in the semi-directive in-depth interviews but not in the pilot enquiry, was re-inserted. The questions on this subject, like those on production, were asked in four stages, covering respectively the preceding four weeks and each of the three crop cycles. The enquiry had five main themes:
   - the umuryango and the inzu (the enlarged family and the conjugal family)
   - the means of production
   - domestic production
   - the household budget and savings
   - attitudes to social change and religious and political socialisation.

D.   The extended family and the conjugal family (The umuryango and the inzu)

The unit for the enquiry was the extended family in its limited sense, "inzu" in Kirundi. (The word "inzu" can also mean the home, the place where the conjugal family lives)[4]. The first questions (1 to 3) concerned the compound, "rugo" in Kirundi, which can house one or

Figure 3
STRUCTURE OF A UMURYANGO: SITUATION A

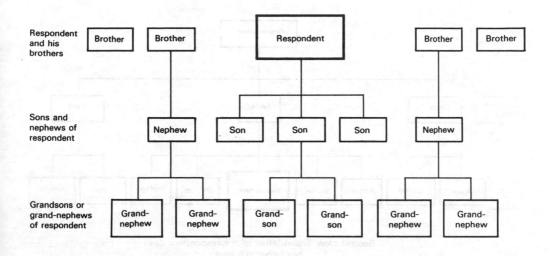

more conjugal families, each with its own separate hut. These questions were aimed at understanding the kinship relations between the different households and the precise position of the respondent in the group as a whole. The next subject was the extended family, "umuryango" in Kirundi, usually scattered, on which the questions in the enquiry were limited to the survival or otherwise of the respondent's ascendants. This restriction was to prevent the interview getting out of hand or overtaxing the respondent's own knowledge. After a filter-question to learn whether the father and/or the grandfather were alive or dead, alternative sets of questions differing only in the terms describing affinity established certain facts about the members of the umuryango according to the position of the respondent in the system of kinship. In cases where neither the grandfather nor the father was still alive (situation A, questions 5 to 15) the umuryango was composed of the kin presented in Figure 3. In cases where the grandfather and/or the father were still alive (situation B, questions 16 to 26) two alternative outlines (Figures 4 and 5) made it possible to establish the pattern of the respondent's umuryango.

Information collected about the umuryango dealt only with the males, since it is they who constitute the economic unit and it is among them that land is shared out at an inheritance, the females being entirely integrated into the family of the male upon marriage. This part of the questionnaire provided essentially the following information: the number, age and marital status of the members of the extended family; migration; social and professional mobility; the area of the land left behind and what had happened to it.

From there on, all the questions concerned only the household itself, consisting of the respondent, his wife or wives, his unmarried children and any relations living with them (grandmother, orphans, etc.). The questionnaire brought out: the history and composition of the household (questions 27 to 36); the origins and geographic movements of the respondent; in cases where the respondent had migrated, the area of the land he had left behind and what

First Case: The grandfather of the respondent still alive

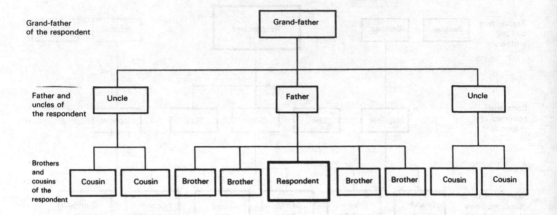

Second case: Grand-father of the respondent dead,
but father still alive

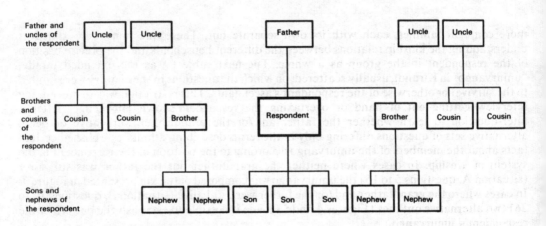

had happened to it; the number, age, sex and education of his children; the kinship relations between the members of the household and the respondent.

E. The means of production

The "means of production" of the household cover the land available to it, the techniques used, the animals, the implements and the labour.

Concerning land (questions 37 to 69, 90 to 93, 97 to 101), the questionnaire obtained: the areas, the way it was acquired, the way it was divided, any transactions (purchase, sale, rental); the social implications of these transactions (the role played in them by kinship, by State organisations, commercial firms, religious communities, etc.); the forms of rent for land rented from or to others; the way in which land had been passed on; title deeds; boundary conflicts; subjective views on the concentration of land ownership.

Concerning production techniques (questions 70 to 89, 94 to 96), the questionnaire tried to establish: the areas of land not used, left fallow or under cultivation, respectively; the order of rotation of crops; fertilizer use; anti-erosion practices; soil fertility; the distribution of land between food crops and cash crops; the use of selected seeds; the extent to which the food needs of the household were met from the land available to it.

The following series of questions (102 to 161) dealt with the animals (large and small livestock, poultry and rabbits). The aim was to make an inventory of the respondent's animals and to determine the social implications of keeping and selling cattle. Other related questions covered by the questionnaire included: views on the concentration of animal ownership, feeding bans (consumption of mutton, eggs, etc.), relations between farming and livestock. Next came a question on the cultural and ideological significance of cattle in the eyes of the respondent.

The ten questions on implements (162 to 171) dealt with their nature, numbers, length of use, and cost, as well as ownership of more elaborate equipment (tractors, attachments, etc.), used by only a small minority of farmers. There was also a question about the hoe and what it represents.

A final group of questions (172 to 225) dealt with various aspects of the use of manpower on the family holding: work done outside the family on other activities (problem of the relationship between the traditional and modern sectors), work done by members of the household, work done by outsiders. This section also included questions on the respondent's education and that of the members of his family, on the forms of wage payment (in cash or in kind), distinguishing between temporary and permanent employment, and on workers' migration.

F.   Domestic production

More than 100 questions (226 to 356) were devoted to the production of the household, making a clear distinction between cash crops and food crops, in accordance with the detailed criteria used in the study, as described earlier. For each of the two types of production, the questionnaire obtained: the total amount of work put in; the physical quantities of produce harvested, consumed in the household and sold, together with the money obtained from sales and the forms of marketing. The impact of cash crops on the farmer, as an index of change, was tackled in a series of questions concerning the share of total cultivated land devoted to them. For food crops, the method and degree of integration of the farmer into the regional market was revealed by means of several questions concerning the amounts of the major food crops harvested and sold. Finally, several questions were devoted to the services provided by outside organisations (insect control, irrigation, provision of machinery, etc.) and to the support and guidance provided by agronomists and extension workers.

G.   The household budget and savings

The household's monetary expenditure (questions 365 to 369) was broken down into two main headings; consumption and means of production. Within consumption expenditure, the questionnaire distinguished between: foods which the farmers could be expected to produce for themselves (cassava, beans, maize, sweet potatoes); superior foods (meat, fish, oil, salt); drinks (native beer, factory-made beer, other drinks); clothing (clothes, footwear); household articles (paraffin, soap, tobacco, batteries, mats, blankets); transport, health (dispensary, hospital, medicine) and education (enrolment fees, stationery, etc.).

Under means of production, the questionnaire covered: expenditure on animals (large and small livestock, poultry); implements and seeds; services of various kinds (insecticides, irrigation, fertilizer, attachments, tractors, rental of fields, etc.); outside labour (temporary or permanent).

Savings were identified in the form of voluntary saving, forced saving and cash hoarding.

H. Attitudes to social change; religious and political socialisation

The final part of the questionnaire was concerned with particular anthropological and sociological aspects, since it covered attitudes to social change and stratification, religious and political socialisation, information and the influence of the past.

Attitudes to social change were revealed by a series of questions (356 to 364) on the idea of a "fair wage", on the education sought for the children, on their professional future and their marriages; views on social and political stratification were derived from answers to questions on the qualities and failings of leaders.

The final set of questions (370 to 395) dealt with religious and political socialisation, information and the influence of the past. The main themes were the religion of the respondent and his relations, attendance at religious ceremonies, explanations for success or failure in agriculture, the causes of disease, frequency of contacts with different levels of authority, political awareness, radio and newspapers, belief in prophets and witch-doctors, and the practice of ancestor-worship in the regions concerned.

I. Relevance of the questionnaire: some criticisms

In spite of its size, the questionnaire used in the quantitative enquiry failed to uncover many significant elements of the process of change in the rural structures in Burundi, while others, although covered in the final version, were insufficiently explored.

The reader will have noticed that the subject of housing, which can be a highly significant indicator of social change, is not among the variables covered by the questionnaire. This is in fact a simple subject to tackle, because all it requires is intelligent observation on the part of the interviewer. The type of hut or house is the most instructive measure of the housing variable. This indicator, by classifying types of house or hut, denotes different material standards of living: for example, in rural areas, the primitive straw hut or the small traditional house with cob walls, a roof of leaves and no woodwork would indicate the lowest level; a house of this second kind, but with one or two rooms and some woodwork (door and/or window), an intermediate level; a permanent structure of brick (of dried earth or baked) with a roof of corrugated iron, tiles or asbestos sheeting, with wooden door and windows and with two or three separate rooms, the highest level. Depending on the requirements of any particular study, this indicator can be refined and amplified by an inventory of the equipment and the furniture, the distance from the road or the main gathering-place, or from the administrative centre of the zone or commune.

Justified criticism can also be made of certain points which, although covered in the final questionnaire, are not dealt with exhaustively or comprehensively. This is true of such aspects as religion, political socialisation, farming or livestock techniques.

Religious beliefs are certainly one of the most difficult subjects to handle in a questionnaire, particularly because of the co-existence of several religions, in which case it is impossible by means of questioning to arrive at the relative weight to be given to each. A respondent may announce his adherence to one of the modern religions and still be bound by a traditional one. For example, a Murundi can practice ancestor-worship (guturekara), or the worship of Kiranga, the legendary mediator between Imana (God) and men, and still be a regular attender at Sunday Mass. The pilot enquiry questionnaire contained more on this subject than the final version, but experience at this stage showed that direct questioning on ancestor-worship or the traditional gods often brought the interview to a halt, because these subjects are tabu. To obtain reliable information, it was necessary to use indirect questions, formulated in such a way as to make the respondent feel that he was not himself involved; similarly for his relations with prophets or witch-doctors, about which he would say nothing. In Ngozi, some composite religious movements have come into existence. An example is Nangayivuza, a sect which mingles elements of Catholicism and traditional practices, although claiming to be far removed from the latter. It was still very active in the North of Burundi in the 1960s[5]. It is clear that socio-economic enquiries using questionnaires cannot grasp the complex phenomenon of syncretism, certainly not when, as in this case, it is severely repressed by the civil and religious authorities, because of the cannibalism, necrophagy and incest involved in its initiation rites, as well as the murders of renegades from the sect, but also and perhaps even more because of its political significance. It is equally understandable that an enquiry of this kind, carried out over a limited period, should be unable to bring out the secular significance of the religious factor.

As for political socialisation, some may wonder why the questionnaire did not give more importance to this question, especially in view of its relevance to the approach used in the enquiry. It could indeed have been extended to the respondent's umuryango in order to find out, for example, how many of the family were professional soldiers (regardless of rank), held office in the State party, etc.. The fact that there were not more questions of this kind is due to the likelihood that they would have caused problems in the interview. The final questionnaire does in fact ask whether any members of the extended or conjugal families are civil servants. Moreover, the sub-group that this would have formed would have been too small to be treated as a separate variable in the multivariate analysis.

The same is true of the attention given to household manufacture. Theoretically, this can provide a measure of integration in the sense that a household which builds its own hut, makes its own tools, its own clothes, its own furniture, is much less integrated into the market economy than one which buys everything on the market. These activities are nevertheless caught, if only indirectly, by the data on the number of tools bought and on the expenditure on goods not produced in the household (certain tools, utensils, clothing, mats, blankets).

The disproportion between the number of questions devoted to agriculture and to livestock may appear surprising. It is true that many elements which would be essential for proper analysis of the profitability and productivity of livestock – and which are mostly available in the case of crop-growing – are not covered in the final version of the questionnaire used in the quantitative enquiry. To carry through an economic input-output analysis of this activity, more detail would be needed on the amount of work put in and on the value of production (milk, butter, manure, weight-gain by cattle). This apparent gap is because the pilot enquiry gave only inconclusive results on the subject. A partial explanation may be that there is little cattle-raising in the regions covered by the study, (only 13 per cent of the farmers in the quantitative study owned large livestock). The importance given to cattle in the study therefore matches their importance in the economy.

The precise wording of any questionnaire can always lead to misunderstandings. This problem can be particularly acute in African countries, where several distinct languages sometimes exist side by side in a limited area. Burundi is fortunate in being in the rare situation, for Africa, of having a single language. There can sometimes be problems, nevertheless. Although the official Kirundi language is the same for the whole country, there are a number of regional variants, which are particularly marked in the East of the country, for example in Mosso and in Ruyigi. In practice, a single Rundi version of the questionnaire was used. Occasional difficulties in understanding certain terms, which virtually only arose in Mosso, were easily solved by the interviewers who came from the areas where the enquiry was taking place. In Ruyigi, for example, where linguistic variations were particularly marked, the interviewers coming from the area were able to help out their colleagues from other regions.

In a multi-disciplinary study of this scope, it is inevitable that everyone, whether agronomist, economist, anthropologist or sociologist, will feel that his own subject has not been done full justice. But an analysis of this size which tries to cover the whole subject could not go further, given the numerous constraints inherent in such a project.

III. FIELDWORK

The success of any enquiry depends on meticulous preparation of the terrain and all the operations taking place in the field. This stage of the research contains eight indispensable elements: the selection and training of the interviewers; obtaining the approval and support of the authorities and the farmers; preliminary contacts; supervision of the interviewers in the hill-districts and the repeat interviews; recording the issue and return of questionnaires; keeping the register of people to be interviewed; the establishment of standard weights and measures; and, finally, the logistics[6].

A. Selection and training of interviewers

The selection and training of the interviewers are always by far the most important aspect of all fieldwork. The interviewer forms the essential link between the researcher and his subject. His role becomes all the more important, the more the researcher finds himself separated from his subject by barriers of a cultural, social, psychological, linguistic or racial character. Moreover, the interviewer must himself be not too far removed, socially, ethnically or culturally, from the respondent, so as to be able to overcome any difficulties of contact or communication.

In spite of efforts to conform to the elementary rules governing methods of enquiry, it turned out to be almost impossible to achieve an ideal combination of qualities in the selection of the interviewers. The ideal situation would have been one in which the interviewers were close to the farming population and living in the interior of the country. Officials in the local administration (typists, secretaries, policemen, etc.) or "officials" from the agricultural authorities (agronomists, extension workers, veterinarians, veterinary assistants), school-teachers, members of religious missions (Sunday School teachers, nurses, secretaries, etc.)

and even some farmers would be among the acceptable categories. These include some people who have successfully completed secondary education, the minimum required for the purposes of the enquiry, but they are rarely found in the interior of the country.

Those with the best training are too valuable for the administrations or other institutions employing them to be made available for a period of several months. Those who are less in demand are often less well-educated and have neither the intellectual capacities nor the interest in the subject needed for work of this kind. The farmers themselves, who would be ideal in many ways, are virtually excluded, because practically all of them are either illiterate or incapable of thinking in abstractions. Nevertheless, the whole of the pilot enquiry was carried out with people from these categories. Experience proved, however, that the subsequent quantitative enquiry required interviewers with much higher standards of knowledge and capacity for abstract thinking. In fact, the pilot enquiry only produced usable results thanks to permanent and intensive supervision (one supervisor to every two interviewers). Moreover, the interviewers coming from a farming background aroused a certain mistrust on the part of some local officials. A different category of person was therefore called in, namely university students. These had the dual advantage of being available during the long university vacation (beginning of July to end of September) and of being capable of classifying answers according to the pre-established categories of the questionnaire. On the other hand, they had the disadvantage of being remote from the rural community and sometimes totally cut off from it. This is why only students from one or other of the three regions of the enquiry were selected, with preference being given to senior students in the economics, agronomy and law faculties, in other words, subjects directly related to the research itself. The interviewers were given an intensive theoretical and practical training in the fortnight before the enquiry. The first step was to provide them with a thorough understanding of the theory and basic concepts involved. Next, the questionnaires were analysed in group discussions, with particular insistence on filter-questions, on the consistency checks to be applied while the interview was still going on and the possibility of asking supplementary questions, on classification methods in the case of certain subjects where difficulties of interpretation could lead to systematic errors (the minimum age for a worker to be considered an adult, the number of days in a working week, weights and measures, etc.), and on certain definitional problems (land in use, land not used, fallow, etc.). The next stage was a series of mock interviews. Farmers were invited to the University, with the students taking turns to act as interviewers. The answers were entered on the questionnaires and whenever a problem of interpretation arose, it was thrashed out in the group under the supervision of the instructors. Finally, there was a test to find out how much of the training had been absorbed. After joint discussions, 47 students were chosen as interviewers.

Over and above careful preparation of each of the approaches to be made, successful fieldwork depends on keeping the whole group sufficiently flexible to deal not only with the unforeseen but also the unforeseeable, since empirical research is a process involving continual readjustment. From another point of view, too rigid a preparation of fieldwork is not necessarily a good thing, because it may lead to harmful silences or breakdowns of various kinds in the interview. The pilot enquiry showed that if the group was to be capable of adapting to changing circumstances, it had to be small in number and given continuous training throughout the period of the enquiry. Too large a group inevitably builds up internal structural rigidities whose inertia hinders continuous adjustment to the invariably rapid evolution of the situation in the field. The answer which was finally found to this problem – after the enquiry had been going on for several weeks – was the creation of geographically separated sub-groups, but the ideal solution was reached only when the number of interviewers was reduced from fifty-odd to about twenty[7].

The brave speeches and the good intentions were rarely lived up to. Ironically, the difficulties encountered in the field came, not from the local authorities, whose contributions and support were on the whole quite generous, nor from the farmers of the hill-districts, whose welcome and hospitality were most benevolent, but mainly from the students, apparently unused to the simple country life – at least at the start of the enquiry – and only faintly interested in the problems of the farmers or the requirements of scientific teamwork, although there were of course a number of praiseworthy exceptions whose devotion to the work was exemplary.

B. Obtaining the approval of the farmers and the authorities

This is an essential part of the procedure, which must be done with tact, but without beating about the bush, in spite of the histrionics displayed by some of the people involved. The scenario must be carefully prepared. At the political level there was no particular difficulty because the climate was favourable at the time to the idea of rural development and to progressive notions of social justice. All that remained to be done was to relate the research to these two themes.

Long before the research started, we were in contact with the Ministère de l'Intérieur, with the authorisation of the Recteur of the University. With the written authorisation of the Ministry – which informed the Governors of the Provinces concerned – and a letter of recommendation from the Recteur, we made contact with the political and administrative authorities of the places selected for our sample. At provincial level, the Governor was informed of the way the research would be carried out and he gave the research supervisors a letter to be passed on to the communal administrators, containing instructions as to the support to be provided. The systematic drawing of lots to decide which individuals would be included in the sample usually took place at communal level, in the presence of the administrator, but sometimes at the level of the zone, depending on whether the register of heads of household covered the commune or the zone. From the point of view of the general conduct of the enquiry, it should be stressed that the choice of farmers to be interviewed was made on strict scientific principles, without any ethnic or tribal preference. The presence of the communal administrator – or the head of the zone – was psychologically beneficial to the enquiry and stimulated collaboration. It was he who, when the lists were being established by the enquiry supervisors, announced the two coordinates in the random numbers table which gave the first name in the register of heads of household which then formed the starting-point for the systematic drawing of lots. Whenever possible, this list was drawn up three days before the first visits by the interviewers. The administrator then sent it by runner to the head of zone who passed it on to the head of the hill-district in the enquiry, who in turn was responsible for convening the farmers whose names appeared on the list, according to the work plan of the enquiry.

Obtaining the support of the farmers was a more delicate matter, because the Murundi peasant is very suspicious of anything emanating from outside his world and in particular of the town-dwellers, always so free with promises they never keep. This approach was made easier by a fortunate combination of circumstances. The President of the Republic on a recent visit to the farmers of the area had abolished personal taxes. The justification for the enquiry was presented to the farmers in the following light:

   i) the young people coming to visit them were students from the University of Burundi and in no way officials of the Administration;

ii) they all came from the interior and were therefore the farmers' "brothers", and were keenly interested in improving the farmers' lives;

iii) if an effective contribution were to be made to efforts in favour of agricultural development, it was necessary to start a dialogue in order to have a clearer idea of the farmers' living conditions and problems so that practical suggestions could be made to the national authorities;

iv) for this reason, the farmers were being asked to speak frankly without giving any false facts or figures;

v) once the interviews in the field had been completed, total confidentiality was guaranteed – the name of neither the farmer nor his hill-district would appear in the official papers to be written following the end of the enquiry.

This manner of justifying the enquiry never failed to have the desired effect.

The actual meeting with the farmers was held at the normal gathering-place. The local administrator responsible for organising the meeting also attended. An official of the communal administration (the administrator, the secretary or the head of zone) or the councillor of the hill-district was responsible for making the introductions. His task was to explain to the meeting the reasons for the presence of the students and for the research. Then a representative of the research group, using the whole panoply of appropriate compliments and etiquette, addressed the farmers, taking particular care to provide the justification for our research activities, after which he called out the names of the farmers selected and introduced each one to his interviewer. The pair of them then went off together to the farmer's hut. Everything had to contribute to the establishment of mutual confidence. At first, the talk was of this and that, of life in the hill-district, the family, the worries of the moment or day-to-day problems. To give the farmer confidence and a feeling of security, the interview-enquiries took place inside the rugo, in front of or inside the hut, with no strangers present, because of his reluctance to display his wealth in front of another person. The aim was also to allow the interview to take place in familiar surroundings and at the same time give the interviewer an opportunity to form a judgement on the family and its material circumstances and, if necessary, to make on-the-spot verification of the answers provided, either by observation or by questioning other members of the family (wife, children, grandmother). The interview usually took place over a jug of banana or sorghum beer. The farmer offered groundnuts or even sometimes a meal. Cigarettes, rare and highly prized in these regions, were also handed round. Both the friendly welcome and the interest shown in the questions lived up to our highest hopes.

C. Verification methods, supervision of the interview, repeat interview, enumeration of the questionnaires

The enquiry was conducted under the continual surveillance of two or three supervisors, assisted by one or two student interviewers. This surveillance was carried out in the rugo at the time of the interview, either in the form of a brief courtesy visit or as a thorough examination of the answers which had been written down concerning facts which could be verified in the rugo itself (members of the household, cattle, poultry, implements, storage area and stocks, etc.). If in any doubt, the interviewer took advantage of the supervisor's visit to clear up any dubious points. For example, on more than one occasion, both interviewer and supervisor accompanied the farmer to his fields to re-measure them, when there was any inconsistency or doubt concerning the correctness of the figures provided.

From time to time, a repeat interview was carried out by a supervisor assisted by an interviewer from outside the normal group. This used the same questionnaire and repeated the original interview, the main aims being to see whether the farmer gave the same answer to the same question on the second occasion and to judge the quality of the work. The results of the repeat interviews were also used to polish the training of the interviewers throughout the enquiry and, in this way, to convince them of the need for this training.

Any large-scale quantitative enquiry requires a well-defined and perfectly clear system for recording the issue and return of questionnaires and for recording the names of people to be interviewed. This was done by means of a card-index, which experience showed to be a simple and effective system. The job of keeping the cards up-to-date was given to one of the interviewers in each group. Each day he had to write on the cards of each interviewer:

a) in the morning, before the interviewer left for work, the date, the serial number or numbers of the questionnaire or questionnaires distributed;

b) in the evening, when he returned, against each questionnaire number, the name of the place where the interview had been held.

The register of the people to be interviewed was kept up by a supervisor who, the evening before the interview, had to write down the name of the interviewer against the name of each of the people to be interviewed and add the serial number of the corresponding questionnaire. When the enquiry took place, this made it possible to check whether the people figuring on the sample list had indeed been present or had had to be replaced by the reserves.

EXAMPLE OF A CARD MONITORING THE ISSUE AND RETURN OF QUESTIONNAIRES:

Name of interviewer: GUSUGUSU Tharcisse

Date of interview	Serial number of questionnaire	Hill-district
26.7.77	1 040	Ntunda
27.7.77	1 050	Kinganda
.	.	.
.	.	.
.	.	.
etc.	etc.	etc.

EXAMPLE OF A LIST OF PERSONS TO BE INTERVIEWED[1]

Hill-district : MIGEGE

Date of interview : 28 July 1977

Person to be interviewed	Interviewer responsible	Serial number
MUHUTU Déogratias	MUSIBIGI Gédéon	1 083
BAGAZA Ildefons	NTAKYNANIRA Jean	1 084
CAYI	NDABAREMEYE Jean-François-X.	1 085
.	.	.
.	.	.
etc.	etc.	etc.

1. If resources had been available, sampling would have been based on aerial photographs in order to avoid the irregularities and failings of the registers of heads of household kept by the local authorities. This would have made it unnecessary to use lists to convene the farmers. It should be mentioned that in certain regions affected by the events of 1972, the word "list" has left very unpleasant memories.

D. Weights and measures

Units of measurement raised particularly thorny problems. The first questionnaire (for the pilot enquiry) used only three units for each crop – for beans, the kilo, the dish and the sack, and for other products, the kilo, the basket and the sack – but these were found to be totally inadequate.

The notion of the kilo is foreign to the farmer and is never used for food products. These are measured in small, medium and large baskets or even sometimes in small or large sacks. To enable each interviewer to carry out an on-the-spot check of the plausibility of the answers concerning amounts harvested, consumed or sold, a special summary table for each major food product was added at the end of each series of questions.

To estimate surface areas, the pilot enquiry had used either the square metre, the hectare, the number of paces up and down and across the field, or the number of "ibivi" or of "ibitara". Like the kilo, the notions of square metre or hectare mean nothing to the farmers of Ngozi and Ruyigi, but the square metre is widely accepted in the plain. The "ibivi" and "ibitara" are traditional measures of area. An "ikivi" (the singular of "ibivi") corresponds to the area which an adult male can "cultivate" in a working day (at the season of preparation of the fields); an "igitara" (the singular of "ibitara") corresponds to a standard area of coffee, introduced in colonial times.

The ikivi is a difficult measure to use because its actual area varies widely, depending on the soil, the strength, age and skill of the cultivator, etc. The results of the pilot enquiry – and comparison with the areas measured by the number of paces – showed that the "ikivi" could be twice as large in one region as in another. Unlike the ikivi, the value of the "igitara" is uncertain because its use has never been entirely accepted.

What the pilot enquiry did establish was that the number of paces provided a usable measure of area. This technique is widely used for property transactions. In the interior, the number of paces along and across each field is generally known, except sometimes in the case of land which has been inherited. When these figures were not carried in the farmer's head – this was often true of the more traditionally-minded farmers – the respondents took the measures themselves by pacing out their fields. It might be thought that these measures, too, would be somewhat suspect, since the length of a normal pace depends on height. On the contrary, experience showed that the pace has in its own way become a standard unit. On many occasions, it was noticeable that the shorter farmers took pains to lengthen their stride in order to arrive at the same measure as the taller ones. It was both amusing and instructive to watch one Ngozi farmer pacing out his steeply-sloping fields. When he had to measure out a distance going up a steep field, he strode out as best he could to respect the standard length. If he slipped, he was meticulous in retracing his steps in order to arrive at an accurate measurement. This farmer, who could write, paced his fields carrying a ball-point pen – borrowed from the interviewer – and a banana leaf, on which he carefully wrote down the measurements.

Profiting from all the lessons learned from the pilot enquiry, we also carefully examined the whole question of weights and measures of volume. The main concern was to be able to classify facts and compare them. It was therefore indispensable, from the point of view of sound scientific method, to derive unique standards applicable to the whole field of enquiry. In this particular case, we needed to obtain as accurate an idea as possible of what was meant by a small, medium or large basket, a small or a large sack, or a medium, large or giant jug of the local beer. In a farming community where there is no industrial centre supplying all the needs of the region or the country, baskets and jugs are made mainly in certain farming households of the hill-district. This can lead to wide divergences in the weights and measures applied, even

Table 49.   Standard weights[1] in kg, of baskets and sacks of food crops,
as observed on the markets of the three regions of the study

Food crop[2]	Type of basket or sack	Bubanza Peasant community markets: Rusizi plain	North Ngozi Mwumba-Kiremba-Marangara	South Ngozi Ruhororo-Rango	Ruyigi Bweru-Ruyigi-Musongati	Kinyinya	Rutana
Cassava:	Basket:						
	large	50	30	48	50	47	50
	medium	30	18	24	35	27	30
	small	22	14	12	25	16	18
	Sack:						
	large				50		50
	small				30		30
Sweet Potatoes:	Basket:						
	large	54	28	45	30	50	45
	medium	36	17	30	25	38	25
	small	18	13	15	15	15	18
	Sack:						
	large				50		50
	small				30		30
Maize (on cob/ in grains)[3]	Basket:						
	large	–	25	24	50	45	50 (45)
	medium	30	15	16	35	30	25 (20)
	small	18	12	8	20	14	18 (15)
	Sack:						
	large	(120)			50		50
	small	(30)			30		30
Beans:	Basket:						
	large	45	50	54	80	80	70
	medium	35	30	36	50	30	40
	small	17	23	18	30	18	25
	Sack:						
	large		100	100	100	100	100
	small		30	36	30	20	25
Sorghum:	Basket:						
	large	45	45	45	70	57	70
	medium	27	27	27	40	20	40
	small	13	21	21	25	14	25
	Sack:						
	large		80	80	80	–	80
	small		29	29	25	23	25
Groundnuts:	Basket:						
	large	40					40
	medium	26					24
	small	17					19
	Sack:						
	large	55					40
	medium	–					30
	small	–					10

1. The standard weights shown in the table give for each food crop the average obtained from a large number of weighings on several markets in each of the communes covered by the enquiry. For example, in the Rutana commune, the standard weights for cassava (large basket, 50 kg; medium basket, 30 kg; small basket, 18 kg) were obtained from 19 weighings for each type of basket carried out on different markets of the hill-districts of Kivoga (4 weighings), Nyamure (5), Nyanzuki (3), Rongero (5) and Rushemeza (2). It should be stressed that the weighings on all the markets were carried out with the same set of scales, part of the equipment of the field group.
2. The table shows only the most widespread food crops in the three regions of the enquiry. Data for numerous other crops (peas, potatoes, ragi, taro) were also collected in the interests of the enquiry.
3. The standard weights for maize in grains are shown in brackets.

though they may be given identical names. The system of weights and measures is, after all, itself one further aspect of local culture. Divergences can in fact indicate different stages of social evolution or transformation.

The kilogram of cotton or coffee is an easily understood notion for the producers, since these crops are weighed at the time of sale and paid by weight. The small and the large sack are industrial products, often imported, and represent a uniform weight throughout the country for identical products. In contrast, the volumes or values represented by baskets or jugs, made in the family or by craftsmen, differ widely from place to place.

In the early days of the enquiry, an attempt was made to find out from the councillors of the hill-districts, for each type of food crop, the weight of the contents of each type of basket and the capacity of each type of jug. This failed because the councillors themselves did not know the answers. Other techniques had to be used. It was hardly practicable to equip each interviewer with a pair of scales for this purpose. Nor would it have been very useful, since the enquiry was taking place in the dry season, when there were hardly any food products in the hut to be weighed. For this reason, a supervisor, assisted by an interviewer, made systematic comparative studies, in parallel with the main enquiry, on the markets of all the communes covered by the study to find out for each food product in the region the standard weight for each type of basket and sack (Table 49).

The capacities of the different types of jug (small, medium, large and giant) were arrived at by the same general method, but with variations according to region (Table 50). In Ruyigi, the contents of beer-jugs are not known either in terms of litres or of bottles of industrial beer. Moreover, on the markets of the interior, the litre bottle is almost unknown, the local beer being sold by the industrial-beer bottle of 0.72 litres, whether for sale or for consumption on the spot. The standard capacities of different types of jug were calculated by taking the receipts from the sale of a full jug and dividing by the price of an individual bottle. In Ngozi the technique was the same, although here the farmer was in fact often able to give the capacity of his jugs in terms of beer bottles. In the plain, almost all the farmers were able to give the exact capacities of the jugs.

Table 50. **Standard capacities, in litres, of beer-jugs, as observed on the markets of the three regions of the enquiry**

Type of beer-jug	Bubanza Peasant community markets	North Ngozi Markets in the communes of:	South Ngozi	Ruyigi Markets in the communes of:		
	Rusizi plain	Mwumba-Kiremba-Marangara	Ruhororo-Rango	Bweru-Ruyigi-Musongati	Kinyinya	Rutana
Jug:						
giant	–	91	72	–	–	95
large	55	36	36	30	50	30
medium	45	24	27	23	30	23
small	23	18	18	18	20	18

Once the standard weights and measures had been established, they were made known to all the interviewers, who then applied them uniformly for measuring amounts harvested as well as sold. The divergences between the systems used in Ruyigi and Bubanza, with Ngozi in an intermediate position, are a fair reflection of the way in which traditional peasant society persists or regresses, depending on the nearness to the capital.

111

CONCLUSION

There can be no real conclusion to this account of the methodology of this enquiry into an impoverished rural milieu, since, despite all our efforts to adapt it, the theoretical model used remains tainted by our Western mentality. Nevertheless, all the techniques applied were adjusted to make them operationally relevant, implying that the approach was not decided by chance, but was a deliberate choice based on theoretical and practical objectives and continually reexamined in the light of the facts.

A large amount of information concerning the modalities of the work, but not directly related to the enquiry or its results, will be found in the Annexes. They may provide warning of possible snags facing other researchers looking into this general problem. They are presented as supporting explanations of the operations concerning the collection and processing of the data.

Our research into rural structures in Burundi progressed from a few simple concepts, by way of a host of variables, mostly with a large number of significant values, to a small number of transformed variables – mostly reduced to their essential characteristics – which seemed capable of reconstituting reality in an intelligible way. The complexities of social reality make it necessary to go down to extreme levels of detail and then, with the rich harvest so obtained, work back to a global reconstruction of reality that is at the same time abstract and concrete, and much more meaningful than the initial abstract model.

To illustrate what we mean and to conclude on an interrogative note, if we take the indices worked out for the purposes of the study (described in summary fashion in the Annexes), it would seem that problems are bound to subsist concerning the relevance of the elements used in their composition. In other words, one question is whether these items drawn from the mass of real facts are in fact representative of those facts. The second question is whether each index contains all the elements it should. Only continuous observation of the society over several years could – perhaps – bring an answer.

NOTES AND REFERENCES

1. A similar, but not identical, approach was used by David C. McClelland in "The Achieving Society", D. Van Norstrand Company Inc., New York, 1961; see especially Chapter 3 "Using Children's Stories to Assess Motivation Levels Among Contemporary Nations", pp.70-71 and "Coding the Children's Stories", pp.73-75.

2. Unless more specifically defined, abbreviated terminology is used for the main regions: the plain, the interior (Ngozi and Ruyigi).

3. In Burundi, the hill-district is of great importance and can be considered as the basic unit, since there is practically no such thing as a village.

4. The conjugal family is the group made up of a man, a woman, and their dependent children.

5. Cf. Rodegem, F.M., *Dictionnaire Rundi-Francais,* Annales du Musée royal de l'Afrique Centrale, Tervuren (Belgium), 1970, pp. 547-550.

6. The logistics of the enquiry and the special problems involved, although substantial, will not be dealt with in the main body of the text but in an annex, for the obvious reason that, unlike the other elements discussed here, they do not affect the quality of the research itself, even though they naturally affect the smooth running of the fieldwork.

7. There seems to be a general tendency for the effectiveness of a group of interviewers to decline when it numbers more than fifty, regardless of the continent or the society in which the enquiry is taking place. In this case, the supervisors found themselves faced with strikes and totally unreasonable wage demands (as in the letter dated August 3rd 1977 from the group of interviewers to the supervisors). The interviewers demanded, *inter alia,* bonuses for the distance walked ("It's not God we're working for") or for going into the bush, time off for a midday siesta and food worthy of research workers ("We want to eat like researchers, not like students"). And yet the conditions of work, as well as the highly generous wages, had been discussed with them in detail before they were recruited.

Annex 1

THE PROCESSING OF THE QUESTIONNAIRES

The completed questionnaires had to be tested for internal consistency before being sent for coding – or discarded, if found inconsistent. These are operations which have to be carried out with the greatest care because the success or failure of the research largely depends on them.

THE CONSISTENCY TESTS

In an enquiry on this scale, it is important to check the quality of the questionnaires filled in by the interviewers. The difficulties which they face must be identified before the enquiry has been under way for more than a day or two. The most necessary test of the quality of the questionnaires concerned the interpretation of the replies received. General awareness of the difficulties was achieved by presenting concrete and precise examples to the group as a whole. The results of the consistency tests made it possible to rank the interviewers in terms of the quality of the work done, and so concentrate the continuing training effort on those who seemed to require it most. The consistency tests also permitted an assessment of the degree of comprehension of the questions on the part of the respondents and to see whether their replies corresponded to actual facts. These tests brought out the inconsistency of certain replies and enabled corrections to be made by re-asking certain corrective questions on the spot. (Some of the tests were built into the questionnaire itself to act as a permanent reminder.) In this way, the interviewer was himself responsible for checking the consistency of the more fundamental facts obtained through the enquiry[1].

In addition, a group which had been specially trained in verification methods applied 82 pre-planned consistency tests to each of the questionnaires. These more far-reaching tests and verification measures by a specialised group made it possible to sort out the usable questionnaires from the unusable before proceeding to coding. Out of 1 655 questionnaires, 67 were rejected for multiple and repeated inconsistencies.

DESIGNING THE CODING

A total of 1 588 questionnaires containing 395 questions and 2 631 possible answers means something like 4 million items of information. Processing such a mass of data can obviously only be done by a computer, and this requirement had been allowed for at the time of drafting of the final questionnaire by including a coding system in the questionnaire itself.

The pre-coding in the final questionnaire was arranged to meet the requirements of the computer installed in the Centre National de l'Informatique in Bujumbura, which used 96-column cards. The pre-coding envisaged that each questionnaire would need 57 of these cards. The information gathered by the enquiry went well beyond the scope of the pre-coding, however, so that numerous additional codes had to be included, over and above those of the enquiry questionnaire. In the end, therefore, 70 cards had to be used for the coding.

THE CODING PROCESS

The coding process consists simply of transcribing the replies contained in all the questionnaires onto special forms which are themselves then transcribed onto whatever data base is used by the computer (punched cards, magnetic tape or discs).

Any enquiry using a questionnaire contains two types of question: those where the replies cannot be pre-determined and those where the range of replies is foreseen in advance – known as open and closed questions, respectively. The questions are necessarily open when the subject is largely unknown territory, and preferably closed when it is more familiar. In a quantitative enquiry, the open questions are kept to the absolute minimum. Between these two extremes there is also the possibility of using open-ended questions, where a certain number of replies are foreseen in advance, but space is left for a final "other" category, to cover replies which fall into none of the pre-determined categories.

In the industrialised countries, where considerable documentation is available, the questions can almost all be closed, but in Africa the lack of basic information makes it necessary to use many more open questions, as was the case in our enquiry. The information in the handful of technical reports available was too fragmentary concerning the rural milieu and was essentially limited to the projects carried out with foreign technical assistance; hence the large number of open and open-ended questions included in the quantitative enquiry.

Coding is a purely technical process which ought to present no problems to staff capable of exactitude and respect for professional standards. Unfortunately, these qualities were difficult to find in this enquiry. About fifty coders recruited from students at the University carried out this first phase of the operation in about two months, but much too unreliably. To correct their errors and inaccuracies – which occurred despite the presence of conscientious and experienced supervisors – a limited group of more carefully chosen students then worked for several months on the coding, with the supervisors themselves coding the open questions. The whole job was submitted to three successive verifications, covering all the replies transcribed onto the coding forms.

Annex 2

PROCESSING THE DATA

Computer treatment of the data was essential not only because of the sheer mass of information acquired but also because of the volume and complexity of the analyses to be made. This processing took place in four stages: data storage on magnetic tape, programming of the uni-dimensional analysis and examination of extreme values, transformation of the original variables, creation of indices and multivariate analysis. This handling of the data requires specialised staff: programmers, punched-card operators, technical staff at the electronic centre, etc.

DATA RECORDING

The coding used in the final version of the quantitative questionnaire was originally planned so that the processing could be handled by the Centre National d'Informatique in Bujumbura. All the coding was therefore planned in relation to 96-column punched cards. But it turned out that the sheer volume of information prevented it from being handled by the computer in the Centre[2]. It was therefore necessary to find another data processing centre in Europe, with the added difficulty that the cards used there are different in format, having 80 columns. The problem was solved by the Centre de calcul électronique of the Swiss Federal Administration in Berne, which took the data from the punch forms and put them straight onto magnetic tape[3]. Data storage on magnetic tape involves a considerable amount of work.

UNI-DIMENSIONAL ANALYSIS

Uni-dimensional analysis is the prelude to multivariate analysis. Even before obtaining the first results of the uni-dimensional analysis, however, the programmer had to rearrange the data coded on the coding forms to fit the order of the questions on the questionnaire. This re-arrangement was made necessary by the number of additional codes introduced in order to accommodate the additional items of information which had not been foreseen at the time of pre-coding. The uni-dimensional analysis provided the whole of the raw data for each of the 2 631 variables and, for each of them, the various measures of dispersion: mean, median, kurtosis, extreme values, skewness, standard deviation, variance, ranking. Those extreme values which seemed abnormal because they fell outside the main body of replies were checked against the corresponding questionnaires, to see whether they were correct or the result of coding error.

Examination, variable by variable, of the initial results of the uni-dimensional analysis made it possible to reduce the number of qualitative values for a great number of variables and to eliminate certain variables which gave no significant results. For example, the original thirty values for the variable on the socio-professional mobility of the members of the umuryango (extended family), were first compressed into six (labourer, employee, farmer/stock-raiser, entrepreneur/trader, student, other) and finally into two (farmer, non-farmer).

The original 2 631 variables were reduced by this process to 564 transformed variables. Of these, 129 were chosen for the multivariate analysis, the final stage in the achievement of the scientific objective.

THE CONSTRUCTION OF THE INDICATORS

The partial reconstitution of reality is achieved by using several original variables in order to construct a large number of indicators. Each of these indicators is obtained by combining a number of original variables, tens or even hundreds in some cases. This is true, for example, of the index measuring the net income of the respondent's household, which is one of the most complex constructions, using 353 original variables.

The following summary of the way some of these indicators are constructed will serve to demonstrate the complexity of the processes applied in order to grasp all the variants of reality, starting from precise, detailed data.

1. The gross income of the household

The gross income of the household is broken down into four main headings:
- the monetary value of total agricultural production (food crops and cash crops);
- receipts from sales of livestock:
  - large livestock
  - small livestock
  - poultry, rabbits
- income from land rented to others;
- earnings of members of the household working outside the family holding.

Each of these headings itself consists of a number of sub-items, each of them itself made up of several elements (Figure 6).

2. Net income of the household

The net income of the household is derived from the gross income by deducting:
- payments in cash or in kind to workers from outside the household;
- payment in cash or in kind for land rented from others;

117

Figure 6

INDICATOR OF GROSS HOUSEHOLD INCOME

Part 1: Agricultural income

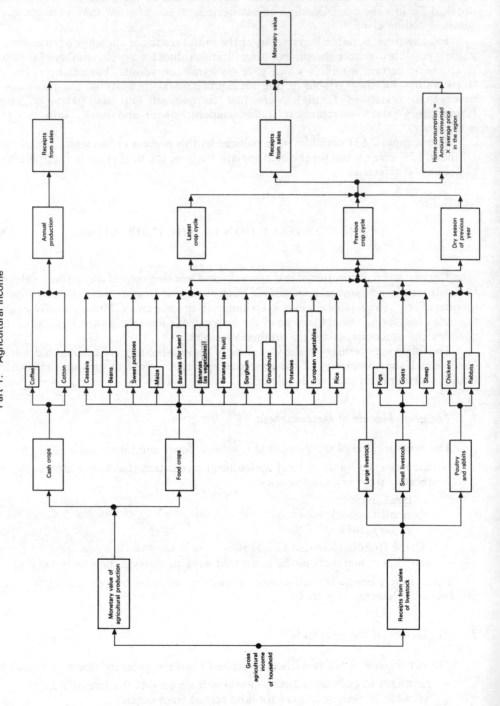

Figure 6

INDICATOR OF GROSS HOUSEHOLD INCOME

Part 2: Non-agricultural income

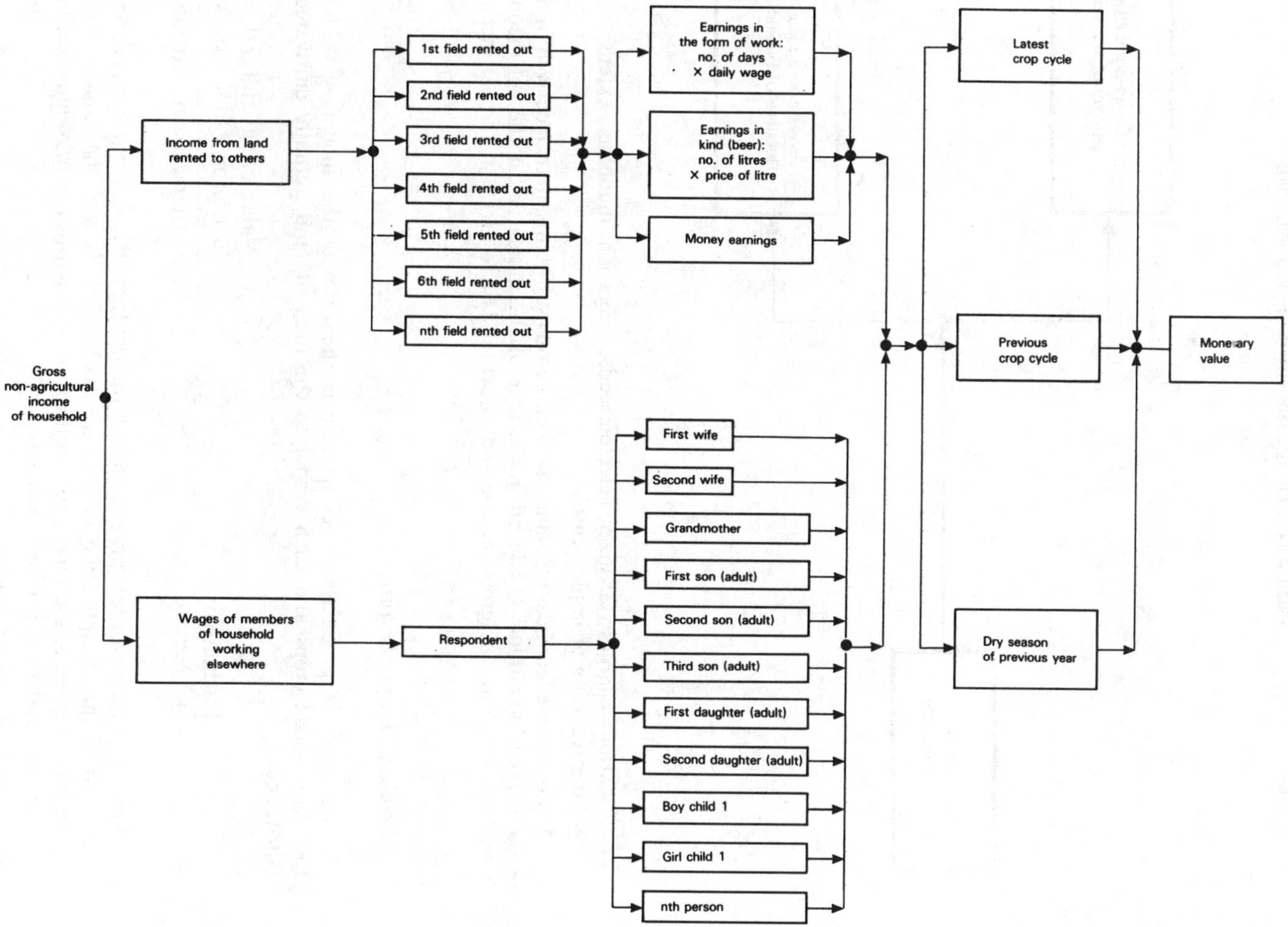

Figure 6
INDICATOR OF GROSS HOUSEHOLD INCOME
Part 3: Total

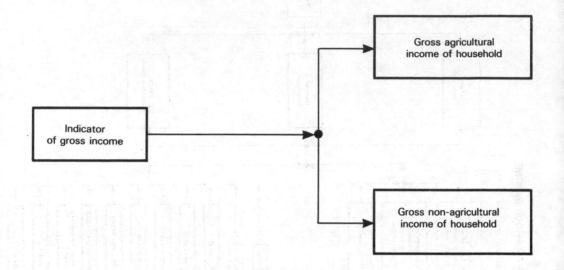

- various charges (fertilizer, selected seeds, irrigation, machines, extension);
- depreciation of implements[4].

Each of these four headings consists of numerous sub-items, in turn derived from a series of the original variables, 353 in all in the case of the indicator for the net income of the household – 186 for the gross income and a further 167 to arrive at the net income.

3. *Productivity per hectare*

The index of productivity per hectare is the ratio of the monetary value of total production (food crops and cash crops) to the area of land actually cultivated by the respondent:

$$\text{Productivity per hectare} = \frac{\text{Value of agricultural production in FBU} \times 10\ 000}{\text{Area of land under cultivation}}$$

This indicator measures only the agricultural productivity of the farmer's holding, taking no account of the receipts from sales of livestock[5]. This is why the value of agricultural production is related to the land under cultivation and not to the total land available.

The area under cultivation is the sum of:

- land under food crops
- land under cash crops.

120

The area of land under food crops consists of:

- land devoted to food crops grown in isolation
- land devoted to combinations of food crops.

The area devoted to food crops grown in isolation includes the land being used for the following products:

Cassava, beans, maize, sweet potatoes, groundnuts, peas, bananas for eating as vegetables or fruit, bananas for beer, bananas (unspecified), sorghum, ragi, soya, taro, rice, potatoes, European vegetables and other food crops.

The land under cash crops is made up of:

- land under coffee
- land under cotton.

4. *Productivity per adult worker*

In the calculation of the index of productivity per adult worker, the total value of production of the holding was related to the number of workers on the respondent's holding.

$$\text{Productivity per adult worker} = \frac{\text{Value of agricultural production plus receipts from sales of livestock}}{\text{Number of adult workers}}$$

The number of adult workers is made up of:

- members of the household working on the holding
- workers from outside the household.

Children aged 15 or under working on the holding were each counted as half an adult.

5. *Capital intensity*

The index of capital intensity of each holding was derived from the monetary value of the implements used by the respondent, related either to the number of hectares of cultivated land or to the number of adult workers.

The starting-point for the calculation of capital intensity was in all cases the monetary value of the dead stock, obtained by multiplying the number of implements owned by the respondent by the unit value of each type of implement. The sum of these values for all the categories defined the monetary value of the dead stock, in other words the capital invested in implements by the respondent.

$$\text{Index of capital-intensity per hectare} = \frac{\text{Number of implements} \times \text{unit price}}{\text{Number of hectares of cultivated land}}$$

$$\text{Index of capital-intensity per adult worker} = \frac{\text{Number of implements} \times \text{unit price}}{\text{Number of adult workers}}$$

121

6. *Labour intensity*

The labour-intensity for the respondent's holding was calculated by means of a series of indices all constructed on the same pattern, i.e. the total annual number of hours worked, per hectare of available land, of cultivated land or of land devoted to one or other kind of crop (food crops, rice, coffee or cotton).

Two different methods were used to estimate labour-intensity per hectare of available land:

- the first index was derived from the number of days worked by members of the household or outsiders on each type of crop and for each different type of farming work (tilling, sowing, weeding, harvesting and certain tasks peculiar to coffee – mulching, pruning, insect control – or to cotton – lifting, burning). This index therefore takes account of the number of days effectively devoted to farm work.

$$\text{Index of effective labour-intensity per hectare of available land} = \frac{\Sigma \text{ days spent on each type of crop and on each type of work}}{\text{Total number of hectares of available land}}$$

- the second index was based on the number of permanent adult workers (members of the household or outsiders) present on the holding, multiplied by 300[6]. To this was added the number of days worked by temporary workers (from inside or outside the household). This index makes no distinction between the number of days devoted to farming and to other activities on the holding.

$$\text{Index of theoretical labour-intensity per hectare of available land} = \frac{\Sigma \text{ (number of permanent workers} \times 300) + \text{days worked by temporary workers}}{\text{Total area of available land in hectares}}$$

The labour-intensity per hectare of cultivated land was calculated for food crops, as well as for rice, coffee and cotton, by the following formulae:

$$\text{Labour-intensity per hectare of cultivated land} = \frac{\Sigma \text{ days worked on food crops, by category of work}}{\text{No. of hectares under food crops}}$$

$$\text{Labour-intensity per hectare of under rice land} = \frac{\Sigma \text{ days worked on rice, by category of work}}{\text{No. of hectares under rice}}$$

(similarly for coffee and cotton).

Clearly, the indices of labour-intensity, like the other indices, provide orders of magnitude rather than precise measurements. It would be an illusion to think that the African farmer, unused to thinking numerically, living by nature's calendar, working with his family in the ancestral way without measuring time, could provide precise indications of the number of days devoted to various tasks.

7. *Exploitation index*

The exploitation index makes it possible to measure the profit which the farmer obtains from using labour from outside the household. Depending on the productivity level of the holding and the size of the payments to outside workers, the respondent may make a smaller or larger profit out of the presence of outside workers on his land. In certain circumstances, he may even lose from it, if the cost of using outsiders exceeds the value of the additional production obtained through their participation in the work of the holding.

Although precise measurement of the actual values of additional production attributable to the work of outsiders is impossible, the data from the enquiry make it possible to calculate, after a fashion, the degree of exploitation of outside workers. This is done by measuring the difference between the average value of the daily production per worker and the monetary value of the average daily wage (in cash or in kind) paid to an outside worker. A positive difference shows the gain, or the degree of exploitation by the farmer of the outside worker; a negative difference means a loss, or the exploitation of the respondent by the outsider.

The calculation of the degree of exploitation involves a whole series of relatively complex steps which can be summarised in three stages as follows:

The first stage is to measure the value of net production per day per adult producer member of the household, through two calculations:

— measuring the net monetary value of the total production of the holding, obtained by deducting from gross monetary value of total production of the holding (value of agricultural production plus receipts from sales of livestock) the operating expenses, i.e.:
    — wage payments to outside workers
    — payments for land rented from others
    — various charges (fertilizer, seeds, insecticide, irrigation, attachments, hire of tractor)
    — depreciation of implements;
— calculating the total number of days worked on the holding by members of the household, made up of:
    — the total number of days worked per year by permanent members of the household
    — the total number of days worked per year by temporary members of the household

The value of net daily production per adult producer member of the household is given by the ratio:

$$\frac{\text{Net monetary value of total production of the holding}}{\text{Total number of days worked on the holding by members of the household}}$$

The second stage involves calculating the average daily earnings of a worker from outside the household, which also requires two steps:

— measuring the monetary value of global remuneration of outside workers, which includes:
    — global annual remuneration (in cash or in kind) of permanent outside workers
    — global annual remuneration (in cash or in kind) of temporary outside workers;

123

- measuring the total number of days worked per year by outside workers, which includes:
  - the total number of days worked by permanent outside workers
  - the total number of days worked by temporary outside workers

The daily average remuneration of a worker from outside the household is then given by:

$$\frac{\text{Monetary value of global remuneration of outside workers}}{\text{Total number of days worked per year by outside workers}}$$

Finally, the index of the degree of exploitation (gain or loss realised by the respondent per day worked on the holding by an outside worker) is then given by:

net value of daily production by an adult working member of the household *minus* daily average remuneration of a worker from outside the household.

The exploitation index therefore indicates the exploitation of the outside worker by the farmer or vice versa. The actual calculation method is composed of a number of steps whose complexity is only partially indicated in the above description[7].

A final remark is needed concerning the calculation of the days worked by temporary workers. In their case, for both the members of the household and the outside workers, days were counted not only by season but also by month. In the case of the permanent workers – outsiders or household members – a uniform calculation was made on the conventional basis (confirmed by enquiry) of 300 days in the farming year.

8. *Index of use of techniques*

This index measures the extent to which the respondent made use of certain agricultural techniques to improve production. Three techniques were taken into account in its calculation: use of fertilizer and/or manure, use of selected seeds, and anti-erosion practices. Four values were recorded, each corresponding to a different level of application of techniques in the farmer's management of his holding:

1. The respondent used none of the techniques
2. The respondent used one of the three techniques
3. The respondent used two of the three techniques
4. The respondent used all three techniques.

9. *Index of home consumption (IHC)*

The degree of home consumption in the household of the respondent was also examined from two different aspects:
either
- the percentage of total cultivated land that is devoted to food crops, i.e.

$$\text{IHC area} = \frac{\text{Area devoted to food crops} \times 100}{\text{Total area of cultivated land}}$$

or

– the percentage of total monetary value of production of the holding (food crops and cash crops) accounted for by the production consumed by members of the respondent's household, i.e.

$$\text{IHC production} = \frac{\text{Monetary value of home consumption of food crops} \times 100}{\text{Monetary value of total agricultural production}}$$

IHC area is not a faithful indicator of the household's degree of home consumption, because the food produced is not always consumed within the household. A large or small part is often sold on the local market. In any case, this index is relatively unimportant from an analytical point of view, being the complement of the integration area index (see 10 below).

IHC production, on the other hand – which is not the complement of the integration production index – is a more refined and more accurate indicator of the subsistence economy. Its calculation involves a large number of steps. The monetary value of home consumption is calculated for each food crop as the difference between the amounts harvested and the amounts sold, multiplied by the average price in the region concerned.

10. Integration into the world economy (IIWE)

The degree of integration of the respondent's holding into the world economy (IIWE) is measured in two different ways:
either

– by the percentage of the total cultivated land which is devoted to export cash crops (coffee, cotton, tea):

$$\text{IIWE area} = \frac{\text{Area under cash crops} \times 100}{\text{Total cultivated area}}$$

or

– by the percentage of the total monetary value of agricultural production (food crops and cash crops) which is accounted for by the receipts from sales of the cash crops (coffee, cotton)

$$\text{IIWE production} = \frac{\text{Monetary value of production of cash crops} \times 100}{\text{Monetary value of total agricultural production}}$$

11. Index of household expenditure per head

This index is derived from the global expenditure of the respondent's household and the number of people it contains:

$$\text{Household expenditure per head} = \frac{\text{Global expenditure}}{\text{Number of people in household}}$$

125

Global expenditure is made up of:

- expenditure on consumption goods
- investment expenditure on capital goods and other farm costs

Consumption expenditure consists of the following categories:

Staple food crops
Other foods
- meat
- fish
- oil
- salt
- other
Beverages
- native beer
- industrially-produced beer
- other
Clothing
- women's clothing
- children's clothing
- the respondent's clothing
- footwear
Miscellaneous

- paraffin
- soap
- tobacco
- batteries
- mats
- blankets
- other
Transportation
Education/health
- dispensary, medicines
- school expenses.

Investment expenditure on capital and other farm costs is made up of the following categories:

Livestock
- large livestock
- small livestock
- poultry/rabbits
Implements
Seeds
Miscellaneous
- insecticide
- irrigation
- fertilizer/manure
- attachments
- tractor hire
- other

Labour
- permanent workers
  temporary workers.

All categories of household expenditure[8] were collected separately for each of the three cycles of the farming year.

The annual expenditure of the respondent's household provided material for the calculation of a large number of indicators. For example, investment expenditure related to the number of hectares of cultivated land is an indicator of the efforts made by the farmer with respect to both livestock and agriculture.

12. Index of the outward-lookingness of the household

The phenomenon of "outward-lookingness" is reflected in the amount of work done by members of the household other than on the family's own land. The index used to measure this is the ratio between the quantity of work, if any, which they do away from the family's land and the total amount of work they do, both on and off it:

$$\text{“Outward-lookingness” of the household} = \frac{\text{Number of days worked off the family holding}}{\text{Total number of days worked, either on or off the holding}}$$

This index is one of those which reflect the transition from a pre-capitalist to a capitalist social structure.

13. Tradition

Somewhat paradoxically, the index used to measure the degree of modernisation in fact measures the strength of tradition, even if this flies in the face of those modernists who set store by the elements of modern civilisation (literacy, mass media, consumption of manufactured goods, etc.). Our indicators are more related to traditional society. The five elements used in the calculation of this index are those which show greater or less attachment to tradition:

- consumption of mutton (a very strong traditional food tabu, connected with traditional belief in Imana, the supreme being);
- worship in honour of Kiranga (mythical and legendary character who mediates between Imana and man);
- the practice of "guterekera" (traditional worship of the spirits of one's ancestors to bring peace and protection against the vindictiveness of the spirit world);
- belief in the witch-doctors of the region and use of traditional medicine.

The index of tradition proved difficult to use in practice. This is why no detailed description is given of its calculation.

The greatest reserve must be attached to this index, which is distorted by various extraneous factors. In the final analysis, it really covers more than the tradition it is intended to measure. In rural areas, there are considerable inhibitions about discussing these phenomena. This is why the questions had to be formulated indirectly to make it easier, or indeed even possible, for some answers to be given, even if this meant that the relevance of the answers suffered as a result. Moreover, correlation of this variable with others gave very few results. It must therefore be used with prudence.

However elaborate the method of calculation of the indices briefly described in this Annex, there is always the problem of the relevance of the elements chosen for their construction. In other words, the primary question must always be whether the facts selected out of the mass of observable reality are truly representative of that reality. The second question is whether the indices contain all the necessary elements. Only continuous observation of the society in question over a long period could provide answers to these questions.

THE MULTIVARIATE ANALYSIS

Multivariate analysis is the process which consists of simultaneously relating several variables to one another and examining their inter-relationships. It involves the use of a battery of techniques for examining the relationships among the empirical data emerging from the enquiry. Only those techniques which were actually used are described here. The three main ones were:

- factorial analysis;
- multiple regression; and
- breakdown[9].

The choice of technique depends partly on the type of variable concerned (qualitative, ordinal or numerical).

Factorial analysis makes it possible to examine the effects of several variables on a given phenomenon and to determine the importance of each of them. By this method, the variables can be listed in order of the influence they exert. It is then possible to eliminate those of lesser importance and to proceed to analyse only the more influential variables. It should be stressed that this method does not identify the phenomenon on which the variables exert their simultaneous but unequal influence. That is determined by the working hypotheses derived from previous theoretical considerations. This type of analysis has therefore only a partial and limited value.

Regression analysis is a second method for examining the inter-relationships among variables. The presence or absence of a relationship between two variables, and its strength, can be portrayed in a scatter diagram. The aim of this technique is to determine the nature of the link between a dependent variable and a number of independent variables.

"Breakdown" was the third type of analysis used. This consists of finding out, as a first step, whether there is a relationship between two variables – one dependent and the other independent – and then seeing whether the relationship still holds when a third variable is introduced, then a fourth and so on, and whether any of these taken by itself also has a significant influence on the phenomenon under examination. This technique makes it possible to say which out of a range of factors is the most important in explaining a given phenomenon.

Annex 3

THE LOGISTICS

The logistic problems encountered during the study cannot be overlooked, because they reflect an aspect of reality and reveal a certain mentality which has to be taken into account before launching any enquiry of this kind. They also demonstrate the size of the gap which can exist between the conditions in which the enquiry takes place in different areas.

The logistic requirements for successful fieldwork are highly varied in nature and need meticulous attention. The importance of these strictly practical aspects should never be under-rated, because in their own way they can decide the success or failure of the whole undertaking. Essentially, they consist of the printing of the questionnaire, the means of transport, the housing and feeding of the interviewers.

THE PRINTING OF THE QUESTIONNAIRE

Secretarial work and the printing of the questionnaire present few problems in developed countries but can be very difficult elsewhere. Qualified and conscientious staff are needed for typing in the vernacular language, but even when the typing has been completed and checked, there remain the printing and assembly of the questionnaires. Printing, done by offset, was easily handled, but the assembly brought several awkward surprises. In this particular case, it became necessary to check the page-numbering of each questionnaire, once it became clear that this could not be left to the State printing service. The checks carried out at the printer's before delivery still left more than half the questionnaires with pages either missing or out of order. This was put right later. It is desirable to have the complete set of questionnaires verified and ready well in advance of the start of the enquiry in order to avoid breakdowns and irritating and costly upsets. Moreover, late delivery of questionnaires can mean complications lasting throughout the fieldwork stage. A stack of defective questionnaires meant an unexpected problem which could only be solved by arduous night journeys over long and difficult tracks between the enquiry site and the capital. It was only through immense efforts of this kind on the part of the supervisors that the enquiry could be brought to a successful conclusion.

TRANSPORTATION

The transport needed to correspond precisely to the number of interviewers and the state of the roads can take the following forms: buses for the periodic trips between the capital and the interior and the daily ones between the group's base and the places where the interviews are to take place; small rugged cars for the movements of the supervisors responsible for overseeing and checking on the interviewers. For our enquiry a Mercedes bus, supplied by the University, carried the whole group on the main access roads. Between the main roads and the meeting-places with the farmers, cars were sometimes used – especially in Ruyigi, where the population is widely dispersed. In spite of all precautions, continual re-planning was needed for certain trips. In Ngozi, for example, it turned out that the weight of the bus exceeded the safety limit of the bridges on some roads (particularly between Kiremba and Maranbara). The immediate problem was solved by hiring a lighter bus (with about twenty seats) on the spot from Ngozi College. The supervisors, who had no particular training in civil engineering, found themselves on several occasions having to take delicate decisions, particularly in the Marangara and Rango communes of Ngozi, concerning the solidity of the bridges which would have to be crossed a few days later in the course of the enquiry and whose planks were sometimes badly eaten by termites.

The cars also helped to maintain continuous liaison between the capital and the area of the enquiry, for such purposes as the return of defective questionnaires to the printer's, the delivery of completed questionnaires to the checking group at the University, bringing questionnaires from the printer's, supplying food or medicines to the interview group, fuel for the vehicles, etc.

The regular maintenance of the vehicles by a mechanic ensured that the progress of the enquiry was not disturbed by transport hold-ups. This work was done by a student familiar with mechanical problems.

HOUSING AND FEEDING THE INTERVIEWERS

In Ngozi and Ruyigi, it was necessary to organise bases from which the group could spread out to do its work.

In Ruyigi, two successive bases were set up: the first at the Ecole Normale in Rusengo, covering the communes of Bweru and Ruyigi, the second at the Foyer Social in the Musongati Mission, for the communes of Musongati, Rutana and Kinyinya. These two centres took charge of housing and feeding the group. (At Rusengo the dormitories and canteen of the Ecole Normale provided good board and lodging. At Musongati, the Polish Carmelite nuns organised a temporary camp in the Foyer Social.) The supervisors, aware of the difficulties resulting from the remoteness of certain hill-districts, proposed setting up a very short-term, two-night, camp in the Butezi area – about 50 kilometres from Rusengo and difficult to reach because of the steep tracks – in order to reach the hill-districts of Solero, Rugati and Nkonowe. But this plan had to be quickly altered because the interviewers claimed that they were unable to sleep on the ground without foam mattresses, even on the dried grass which was in fact particularly suitable for the purpose, and that they were frightened of the presence of witch-doctors, who, they said, were particularly numerous and awe-inspiring. Following this setback, plans for a similar camp in the Kinyinya commune, where some hill-districts are a good day's walk from Musongati and difficult to reach, were also abandoned. In spite of these difficulties, all the hill-districts in the sample were reached from the two main bases, thanks to the determination of a limited number of particularly active interviewers to achieve the aims of the enquiry.

In Ngozi, the interviewers were accommodated successively in three bases: Ngozi College, the Petit Séminaire in Burasira and the Ecole Normale in Bukeye. The coverage of the road system being better than in Ruyigi – probably because of the high population density – everything here was much easier. Two interviews could be made in a day, compared with only one in Ruyigi.

Finally, in Bubanza and for the peasant communities in the plain, the interviewing could be performed from the capital. The interviewers were housed on the University campus. Although the distances were considerable, the enquiry was greatly helped by the comprehensive and well-maintained road system.

Feeding was carried out by the various centres, which were responsible both for supplying and preparing the food. The midday meal was eaten with the local people.

NOTES AND REFERENCES

1. For example, the interviewer had to check for himself the consistency between the total area of land utilised and the total area of cultivated land, between the total area of land under various individual food crops and the sum of the areas recorded for each field devoted to any specific food crop. For each cash or food crop, he also had to check the relationship between the amounts sold and the money received from the sales. It was a simple matter to verify the consistency by applying known prices.

2. The computer of the Centre National d'Informatique in Bujumbura had insufficient capacity to handle the mass of data obtained in the enquiry on rural structures in Burundi. It should be pointed out that the member of the research team concerned had not failed to put this question to the management of the Centre d'Informatique before proceeding to pre-code the final version of the questionnaire. The expert on these questions at the Centre had given the necessary assurances concerning the possibility of computer processing on the spot, but when the time came to record the data, he had to climb down and admit that the Bujumbura computer lacked the capacity to deal with the results of the enquiry.

3. It is interesting to note that an appreciable part of this work was done by a group of operators in Blatten, a small community of mountain farmers in the Loschental, a remote valley in the Valais canton of Switzerland – an example of the contribution which can be made by an under-developed region, but obviously in a developed industrial country.

4. Depreciation on dead stock is calculated with great precision. The questionnaire permitted an inventory of all the implements used by the respondent together with the unit price and the number of months of utilisation, for each category of implement. Depreciation was calculated in terms of the capital value and the average period of utilisation of each category of implement:

$$\text{Annual depreciation for each category of implement} = \frac{\text{Number of implements} \times \text{unit price} \times 12}{\text{Months of utilisation of an implement}}$$

The depreciation on dead stock, an indicator in itself, represents the annual amount of depreciation of all the implements found on the respondent's holding.

5. Another indicator including receipts from livestock sales was constructed to measure productivity per hectare of land available to the respondent.

6. The number of days worked in a year: 300 for an adult, 150 for a child aged 15 or under.

7. A second index was calculated by a different method in order to verify the plausibility of the results obtained from this index of the degree of exploitation.

8. By "household" is meant in this context: the respondent, his wife or wives, his own unmarried children, and other persons (grandmother, orphans, etc.) living with him permanently as members of the family. Children living permanently away from the rugo (as students in the capital or elsewhere) are not included.

9. The technical aspects will be found in the standard publications dealing with techniques for research and statistical analysis in the social sciences: for example, Mayniz, R., Holm, K., Hubner, P., *Einfahrung in die Methoden empirischer sociologie*, Opladen, Westdeutscher Verlag, dritte Aufhage, 1972; or Boudon, R., Lazersfeld, P., *L'analyse empirique de la causalité*, Mouton, Paris, 1966.

OECD SALES AGENTS
DÉPOSITAIRES DES PUBLICATIONS DE L'OCDE

ARGENTINA - ARGENTINE
Carlos Hirsch S.R.L.,
Florida 165, 4º Piso,
(Galeria Guemes) 1333 Buenos Aires
Tel. 33.1787.2391 y 30.7122

AUSTRALIA - AUSTRALIE
D.A. Book (Aust.) Pty. Ltd.
11-13 Station Street (P.O. Box 163)
Mitcham, Vic. 3132   Tel. (03) 873 4411

AUSTRIA - AUTRICHE
OECD Publications and Information Centre,
4 Simrockstrasse,
5300 Bonn (Germany)   Tel. (0228) 21.60.45
Local Agent:
Gerold & Co., Graben 31, Wien 1 Tel. 52.22.35

BELGIUM - BELGIQUE
Jean de Lannoy, Service Publications OCDE,
avenue du Roi 202
B-1060 Bruxelles   Tel. 02/538.51.69

CANADA
Renouf Publishing Company Limited/
Éditions Renouf Limitée Head Office/
Siège social – Store/Magasin :
61, rue Sparks Street,
Ottawa, Ontario K1P 5A6
          Tel. (613)238-8985. 1-800-267-4164
Store/Magasin : 211, rue Yonge Street,
Toronto, Ontario M5B 1M4.
          Tel. (416)363-3171
Regional Sales Office/
Bureau des Ventes régional :
7575 Trans-Canada Hwy., Suite 305,
Saint-Laurent, Quebec H4T 1V6
          Tel. (514)335-9274

DENMARK - DANEMARK
Munksgaard Export and Subscription Service
35, Nørre Søgade, DK-1370 København K
          Tel. +45.1.12.85.70

FINLAND - FINLANDE
Akateeminen Kirjakauppa,
Keskuskatu 1, 00100 Helsinki 10   Tel. 0.12141

FRANCE
OCDE/OECD
Mail Orders/Commandes par correspondance :
2, rue André-Pascal,
75775 Paris Cedex 16
          Tel. (1) 45.24.82.00
Bookshop/Librairie : 33, rue Octave-Feuillet
75016 Paris
          Tel. (1) 45.24.81.67 or/ou (1) 45.24.81.81
Principal correspondant :
Librairie de l'Université,
13602 Aix-en-Provence   Tel. 42.26.18.08

GERMANY - ALLEMAGNE
OECD Publications and Information Centre,
4 Simrockstrasse,
5300 Bonn   Tel. (0228) 21.60.45

GREECE - GRÈCE
Librairie Kauffmann,
28 rue du Stade, Athens 132   Tel. 322.21.60

HONG KONG
Government Information Services,
Publications (Sales) Office,
Beaconsfield House, 4/F.,
Queen's Road Central

ICELAND - ISLANDE
Snæbjörn Jónsson & Co., h.f.,
Hafnarstræti 4 & 9,
P.O.B. 1131 – Reykjavik
          Tel. 13133/14281/11936

INDIA - INDE
Oxford Book and Stationery Co.,
Scindia House, New Delhi 1   Tel. 45896
17 Park St., Calcutta 700016   Tel. 240832

INDONESIA - INDONESIE
Pdin Lipi, P.O. Box 3065/JKT.Jakarta
          Tel. 583467

IRELAND - IRLANDE
TDC Publishers – Library Suppliers
12 North Frederick Street, Dublin 1
          Tel. 744835 749677

ITALY - ITALIE
Libreria Commissionaria Sansoni,
Via Lamarmora 45, 50121 Firenze
          Tel. 579751/584468
Via Bartolini 29, 20155 Milano   Tel. 365083
Sub-depositari :
Ugo Tassi, Via A. Farnese 28,
00192 Roma   Tel. 310590
Editrice e Libreria Herder,
Piazza Montecitorio 120, 00186 Roma
          Tel. 6794628
Agenzia Libraria Pegaso,
Via de Romita 5, 70121 Bari
          Tel. 540.105/540.195
Agenzia Libraria Pegaso, Via S.Anna dei
Lombardi 16, 80134 Napoli.   Tel. 314180
Libreria Hœpli,
Via Hœpli 5, 20121 Milano   Tel. 865446
Libreria Scientifica
Dott. Lucio de Biasio "Aeiou"
Via Meravigli 16, 20123 Milano Tel. 807679
Libreria Zanichelli, Piazza Galvani 1/A,
40124 Bologna   Tel. 237389
Libreria Lattes,
Via Garibaldi 3, 10122 Torino   Tel. 519274
La diffusione delle edizioni OCSE è inoltre
assicurata dalle migliori librerie nelle città più
importanti.

JAPAN - JAPON
OECD Publications and Information Centre,
Landic Akasaka Bldg., 2-3-4 Akasaka,
Minato-ku, Tokyo 107   Tel. 586.2016

KOREA - CORÉE
Pan Korea Book Corporation
P.O.Box No. 101 Kwangwhamun, Seoul
          Tel. 72.7369

LEBANON - LIBAN
Documenta Scientifica/Redico,
Edison Building, Bliss St.,
P.O.B. 5641, Beirut   Tel. 354429-344425

MALAYSIA - MALAISIE
University of Malaya Co-operative Bookshop
Ltd.,
P.O.Box 1127, Jalan Pantai Baru,
Kuala Lumpur   Tel. 577701/577072

NETHERLANDS - PAYS-BAS
Staatsuitgeverij Verzendboekhandel
Chr. Plantijnstraat, 1 Postbus 20014
2500 EA S-Gravenhage   Tel. 070-789911
Voor bestellingen: Tel. 070-789208

NEW ZEALAND   NOUVELLE-ZÉLANDE
Government Printing Office Bookshops:
Auckland: Retail Bookshop, 25 Rutland Street,
Mail Orders, 85 Beach Road
Private Bag C.P.O.
Hamilton: Retail: Ward Street,
Mail Orders, P.O. Box 857
Wellington: Retail, Mulgrave Street, (Head
Office)
Cubacade World Trade Centre,
Mail Orders, Private Bag
Christchurch: Retail, 159 Hereford Street,
Mail Orders, Private Bag
Dunedin: Retail, Princes Street,
Mail Orders, P.O. Box 1104

NORWAY - NORVÈGE
Tanum-Karl Johan a.s
P.O. Box 1177 Sentrum, 0107 Oslo 1
          Tel. (02) 801260

PAKISTAN
Mirza Book Agency
65 Shahrah Quaid-E-Azam, Lahore 3 Tel. 66839

PORTUGAL
Livraria Portugal,
Rua do Carmo 70-74, 1117 Lisboa Codex.
          Tel. 360582/3

SINGAPORE - SINGAPOUR
Information Publications Pte Ltd
Pei-Fu Industrial Building,
24 New Industrial Road No. 02-06
Singapore 1953   Tel. 2831786, 2831798

SPAIN - ESPAGNE
Mundi-Prensa Libros, S.A.,
Castelló 37, Apartado 1223, Madrid-28001
          Tel. 431.33.99
Libreria Bosch, Ronda Universidad 11,
Barcelona 7   Tel. 317.53.08/317.53.58

SWEDEN - SUÈDE
AB CE Fritzes Kungl. Hovbokhandel,
Box 16356, S 103 27 STH,
Regeringsgatan 12,
DS Stockholm   Tel. (08) 23.89.00
Subscription Agency/Abonnements:
Wennergren-Williams AB,
Box 30004, S104 25 Stockholm. Tel. 08/54.12.00

SWITZERLAND - SUISSE
OECD Publications and Information Centre,
4 Simrockstrasse,
5300 Bonn (Germany)   Tel. (0228) 21.60.45
Local Agent:
Librairie Payot,
6 rue Grenus, 1211 Genève 11
          Tel. (022) 31.89.50

TAIWAN - FORMOSE
Good Faith Worldwide Int'l Co., Ltd.
9th floor, No. 118, Sec.2
Chung Hsiao E. Road
Taipei   Tel. 391.7396/391.7397

THAILAND - THAILANDE
Suksit Siam Co., Ltd.,
1715 Rama IV Rd.,
Samyam Bangkok 5   Tel. 2511630

TURKEY - TURQUIE
Kültur Yayinlari Is-Türk Ltd. Sti.
Atatürk Bulvari No: 191/Kat. 21
Kavaklidere/Ankara   Tel. 17.02.66
Dolmabahce Cad. No: 29
Besiktas/Istanbul   Tel. 60.71.88

UNITED KINGDOM - ROYAUME UNI
H.M. Stationery Office,
Postal orders only:
P.O.B. 276, London SW8 5DT
Telephone orders: (01) 622.3316, or
Personal callers:
49 High Holborn, London WC1V 6HB
Branches at: Belfast, Birmingham,
Bristol, Edinburgh, Manchester

UNITED STATES - ÉTATS-UNIS
OECD Publications and Information Centre,
Suite 1207, 1750 Pennsylvania Ave., N.W.,
Washington, D.C. 20006 - 4582
          Tel. (202) 724.1857

VENEZUELA
Libreria del Este,
Avda F. Miranda 52, Aptdo. 60337,
Edificio Galipan, Caracas 106
          Tel. 32.23.01/33.26.04/31.58.38

YUGOSLAVIA - YOUGOSLAVIE
Jugoslovenska Knjiga, Knez Mihajlova 2,
P.O.B. 36, Beograd   Tel. 621.992

Orders and inquiries from countries where Sales
Agents have not yet been appointed should be sent
to:
OECD, Publications Service, Sales and
Distribution Division, 2, rue André-Pascal, 75775
PARIS CEDEX 16.

Les commandes provenant de pays où l'OCDE n'a
pas encore désigné de dépositaire peuvent être
adressées à :
OCDE, Service des Publications. Division des
Ventes et Distribution. 2. rue André-Pascal. 75775
PARIS CEDEX 16.

69482-03-1986

OECD PUBLICATIONS, 2, rue André-Pascal, 75775 PARIS CEDEX 16 - No. 43465 1986
PRINTED IN FRANCE
(41 86 04 1) ISBN 92-64-12803-4